The Goodbye Land

The Goodbye Land

by JOSE YGLESIAS

PANTHEON
BOOKS

A Division of Random House · NEW YORK

First Printing
© *Copyright, 1967, by Jose Yglesias*
All rights reserved under International and Pan-American
Copyright Conventions. Published in New York by Pan-
theon Books, a division of Random House, Inc., and
simultaneously in Toronto, Canada, by Random House
of Canada Limited.
Library of Congress Catalog Card Number: 67-13173
A substantial portion of the contents of this book ap-
peared originally in The New Yorker *in slightly different*
form.
Manufactured in the United States of America
by Vail-Ballou Press, Binghamton, New York
Designed by Jaime Davidovich

For *Georgia Yglesias*

For *Dalia* and *Jose Corro*

The Goodbye Land

1

When I was five, the cigar-makers in the Latin section of Tampa, Florida, held a collection on payday to send my mother, my sister and me to Havana to see my father. Four years earlier, he had become ill with encephalitis—the Sleeping Sickness, they called it then—and when he got over the first attack, he began to wander away from home for the second time in his life. When he was thirteen, he had left the province of Galicia in northern Spain, accompanied by a cousin the same age and from the same tiny *aldea* in the mountains. First, he went to Havana, where he spent four years as an apprentice in a cigar factory, like a young Dickens hero. From there, already the owner of a dark suit with thin gray stripes, high starched collars and a straw hat, he went to Tampa to work in the cigar factories; and at a Wednesday night social of the West Tampa Methodist Church, run by missionaries who quite rightly considered they were bringing the gospel to virgin territory, he met my mother when she was not quite sixteen. They got married and, of course, never went back to church. My grandfather's pleasure at having the youngest and last to marry of his five daughters safely given away was soon dampened by my father's sociable and gay habits: having come of age in Havana, my father liked to stop at the cafe on his way home for his espresso and to return after dinner to talk and play dominoes. Not at all like Grandfather's other Galician son-in-law, a sober-minded man, not given to leaving the house after work, which was what you were to expect of Galicians. Father first got sick on the eve of what was to be the ten-months strike of 1920—a watershed in the Latin community of Tampa, from which a generation now dying out dates most events in their lives —and the crippling fever did not make him as anxious as did his knowledge that he could not be at the factory the next day. He had been chosen by the strike committee for all the factories to get up from his worktable at the secretly appointed hour, and call down the block-long floor of rows of closely packed tables, in a voice that hundreds could hear, "Outside, comrades, outside!" He had already received the folded piece of paper and read the date and the hour he was to do this; he kept it in the back pocket of his brown pants, the one with the button-down flap. Months later, when the strike was over and he could not go back to work because his right hand without warning would open spasmodically, he still kept the piece of paper with him when he left for Havana. He was a member of the

4

Centro Español, a mutual aid society of cigarmakers for which there was a counterpart in Havana, and although the cigarmakers in Tampa had months to go yet before they could pay the grocer's bills accumulated during the strike, they held a collection, as they did for us later, to pay for Father's trip to Cuba: surely the doctors of the Centro in Havana would know how to cure his creeping paralysis. It affected not only his hand but his right leg, which he dragged behind him, and his throat, which would suddenly cause him to stutter or be unable to swallow. The doctors did not cure him, of course, and Father began to believe that if he could once more breathe the air of Galicia and eat the food they grew in their tiny farms along the mountainside, ah if he could do that for a few months, he would surely get well. There was still some money left from the collection, to which he could add the fifteen dollars a month the Centro in Tampa gave Mother and which she passed on to him, so he went back to Galicia to visit his mother and sister in the aldea. His sister had just been widowed, and for a while he helped them work the land, and he answered, *Do not worry*, to Mother's letters reminding him that since he was a resident alien in the States he must return before the year was out. It turned out that Mother was right to worry, for Father contracted typhoid in Spain and did not make it back in time. Weak but desperate, he arranged to be smuggled back to Cuba on the regular liner which left from Vigo, and, like hundreds of others, would have gotten into Cuba illegally had not a recurrence of the typhoid on board ship made him very ill: the ship's officers would not take the

5

risk and turned him over to the Cuban authorities when they came on board on their routine visit. He was transferred to a hospital for infectious diseases in Havana, and that was when Mother (who was twenty-eight and had never been out of Tampa) and my sister and I went to Havana in the hope that we would, somehow, bring him back with us. I remember vividly the slum street where we stayed with Father's uncle; but I did not know that Mother, besides seeing Father at the hospital every day (she took him a bottle of milk because the diet there was bad), spent her time seeing the Cuban authorities, the Spanish embassy, and the American embassy. She took me to the hospital only once, and when I saw my sister run ahead to one of the long rows of beds, I went after her, looked at the man she kissed, and asked if he was my father. He smiled and I jumped on the bed and kissed him too, not to be outdone by my sister who saw him almost every day. He had not shaved in several days and his beard was scratchy; that is all I remember of him, but the story of how I instinctively knew who he was and how eagerly I kissed him has been retold often by my Tampa aunts, always to my glory. Mother failed; neither Cuba nor the United States would have him, and the Cuban authorities were only waiting for him to get over the attack of typhoid or the Sleeping Sickness—they were not sure what he had—to put him on a ship back to Galicia. The Spanish ambassador, who could afford to be candid, told Mother, "Madam, if you or your family were wealthy, you would have no problem with your country's immigration laws." Mother waited until she was sure there was nothing else to be done to tell Father, and then only when the sailing date of his ship was near. "I do not want to go back," he said. "If they put me on that ship, I shall jump overboard when it is in the middle of the ocean. I do not want to live." "Man, what are you saying! You must not be in your right mind," Mother argued. "You know I am going back to Tampa and that our whole family will work to bring you back. We shall write to Washington, you shall see." It was a coincidence that the ship for Spain left on the same day as ours for Tampa. I was sorry that the voyage to Tampa lasted only a day, for we had a cunning little cabin with two berths and I liked the idea of sleeping with Mother in the lower one. When we went to bed, Mother called up to my sister and told us for the first time that Father was on his way to Spain and that she wanted us to pray with her for his safe trip. Then she began to pray, and I was so astonished to hear her speak English that I could not respond. "Our Father who art in Heaven," said Mother, remembering those Wednesday night meetings at the West Tampa Methodist Church, and my sister, who was nine years old and knew English, echoed from the upper berth, "Our Father who art in Heaven." At first I did not like it, and I interrupted Mother to tell her I did not know English, and she said, "That is all right, you listen and wish your father well." Lying on my side, absorbing my mother's warmth and watching the moonlight coming in the porthole, I felt good, and went off to sleep, as on Christmas Eve, certain that when morning came some aunt or uncle or sister or cousin—not Santa Claus—would have made my good wishes come true. Forty years later, in the spring of 1965, I went to Galicia to see the country where my father was born and died, feeling excited at the prospect, emotions which were but a slight resurgence of my childhood feelings, for intellectually I was cool now: I had long ago assimilated the knowledge that the goodbyes of the poor are forever, their ten-months strikes are never won, and the letters they write to Washington are not read but weighed.

My father went back to Miamán, the little aldea on the mountainside, writing seldom and then not at all when the paralysis got worse; after a year, he was good only to take care of the cows, getting up before dawn to lead them up to the forest where, if the flies bit, they would not run into the fields under cultivation. When he could not do that, he lay at home, and when the women could no longer take care of him, they took him to the hospital at Santiago de Compostela; the hospital kept him a few weeks only, until they realized that he was incurable and could only be given nursing care, so they arranged to transfer him to a charity home; there he spent the last three years of his life. Just before I left for Europe in the summer of 1964, I asked Mother what she had heard about his stay there and what was the name of the place. "Well, you can imagine, his mother could not see him often. They were poor and the city was far away. I remember that she said—or the man who used to write the letters for her—anyway, she wrote that he did not talk to her. She did not know whether it was the paralysis or whether he just did not wish to talk." Mother rubbed the

8

lobe of her right ear between two fingers, a habit with her
when pensive, and said, "Your father was a very sociable
man."

Mother came to New York to see me and my wife and
our eleven-year-old son off to Europe, and she brought a
copy of Father's baptismal papers for me; also, the last
letter she received from Miamán, two years after Father
died, announcing the death of his widowed sister. After
that the old woman, which is how we always referred to
Father's mother, never had another letter written to her
daughter-in-law in America; that last letter was written in
1933, so I knew I had no more relatives in Galicia, for the
old woman had never mentioned any. I planned to spend
a year in Spain, however, and I promised my mother and
sister to go to Galicia, look up Miamán, find Father's
grave, and talk to people in the aldea who might remember Father or the old woman; I had a camera and I
planned to take pictures to send back to them in Tampa
and thus lay to rest this ghost which haunted all three of
us.

"And so," I said to Mother, "you did not write again
after the old woman didn't answer your last letter?"

Mother sighed, as if the memory of those years were a
hard rock so imbedded in the past that it was too much to
drag it up now. "Oh no, I wrote several times. Though not
too often, for I liked to send ten dollars or at least five
with each letter and—and, you know."

There it was, the old uncrushable rock of guilt: the old
woman had had an invalid son dumped on her and what
had we done to help? My sister and I had gone over the

situation many times in the past: the old woman had been widowed before Father left Galicia at the age of thirteen, so was her daughter by the time Father returned, life in Galicia was hard, and in her old age the old woman had without warning to take care of an invalid son and a sick daughter. And it had been her terrible task to turn him over to hospitals and charity homes. Charity homes! We knew what they were in our country and could imagine how much worse in Spain. Even after the war, when my sister and I had married and had less pity for ourselves (for anyone could see that we had survived the terrible blow to ourselves) we would often sit out on the porch, after the others had gone to bed, and talk about what must have happened after Father's ship reached Vigo with him still—thank God!—on board. By the time we recounted the last visit the old woman paid him, walking many miles to Santiago only to sit before a mute man who simply stared ahead, we would decide it was foolish to lacerate ourselves that way: we were kids, after all, when it happened, and Mother did send what little money she could find.

One of the reasons we still thought about the old woman after the war was that Mother regularly mailed packages of clothes to a Spanish family in Toulouse. They were one of thousands who crossed into France when the north of Spain fell to Franco's army, and the cigarmakers in Tampa, supporters of the Republic, passed around to each other the names of families in exile now suffering at the hands of the French. Galicia had immediately fallen when the civil war broke out, and often my sister would say, "What a problem! What if Father had lived or the old woman? We would have been sending things to the fascist side!" And when I decided to go to Spain, my sister said on the long-distance phone, "You know—isn't it funny? —you may be able to find records of the old woman and Father because they say nothing was destroyed there during the war. It wasn't like Asturias where people who go back can't find records at the churches or city halls."

We left in October and entered Spain at Hendaye, for we had a week before we were due in Barcelona and there was time to take a quick look at the north before settling down for the winter. I had a year in Spain ahead of me: no need to hurry to do anything. But I did want to see the north first because my family in the main came from there. Besides my father and my Galician uncle, there were uncles who came from Asturias; my brother-in-law had spent several years in a country village in Asturias, and he gave me letters to people there. The Spain that most drew me was not the one everyone has heard about: not Madrid, Barcelona, Andalusia, but Asturias and Galicia. Asturias because it is rebellious, Galicia because it is my father's province.

But the weather was bad, as I had been warned; it was raining when we arrived at the station in Irun, and it continued to rain for a week. The bus I wanted to take to Asturias ran only every other day in the fall, and the Irun hotel, after a modest one in Paris where the bathroom was permanently locked, was good and the hot water plentiful. Our entrance into Spain was inauspicious: Rafael, my eleven-year-old son, looked out the window after we left

Hendaye and said, "It doesn't look any different from France." But it immediately felt different, unexpectedly so: the Civil Guards at the station looked harmless, not darkly ominous as in the Lorca ballad. And although the station was being torn down and a new one being built further down the tracks, everything went smoothly; in France we had to carry our many bags through ten cars without anyone to help us, but in Spain a sweet, round-faced old Basque took us in hand. He got us through customs, checked the bags we would not use, opened checkrooms which were closed for the siesta, and put us in a taxi, all the while telling us about Irun, about the weather—it had been raining for eight days—and welcoming the son of a Spaniard to Spain.

I stood at the hotel window and looked at the rain on the main street of Irun, a terrible impatience welling up in me to be out walking and talking to people. It had not been possible on the train; we were in a compartment with a sleepy middle-class Spanish couple, and it was not until we got out at customs that I realized that elsewhere on the train there were hundreds of Spanish workers going back. They were all nervous and anxious, hanging on to tin valises or packages held together with rope, and they kept reminding one another as we approached the immigration windows, "Hold the passport in one hand, do not forget!" The porter had gone ahead with our bags, so we carried nothing and got a smile at the window, whereas they got a searching, cold look and then had to proceed to long tables where they unwrapped everything they had brought with them. I do not know what the porter said to the customs man, but as soon as we walked away from the window, our passports stamped, the customs man smiled and said, "Americanos?" and cleared our bags by making a chalk mark on each. That was that, and the clusters of Civil Guards along the station platform opened a path for us and the porter, and touched their hands to their shining black patent leather hats.

The porter and the taxi driver confirmed that all those Spaniards had been working in France or Germany or Belgium, and later in Barcelona and Alicante and Madrid railroad stations I was to see many more all clutching their belongings and heading home. They were treated harshly by the customs guards because bureaucrats are that way and because the guards were enviously certain the workers had made their pile abroad, their *cuartos*, and anyway, in those meager packages, neatly hidden, must be a transistor radio and a wrist watch, but especially a transistor, and they must be made to pay. But we were tourists and Americans: the number one industry and the number one friends.

That was a strange feeling, to know in that first-class hotel, where the courtesy of the waiters and the people at the desk served to keep us at a distance, that I had arrived in Spain and was merely a tourist and an American. It was almost a rejection—at least for me: my wife is New York-born of Polish and Russian Jews and my son feels American and nothing else—and the rain seemed to emphasize it. I looked out the window and saw nothing that looked like Spain to me: cement block buildings with shops at the street level, Mussolini architecture. It was, as my sister might have said, funny: funny that we, had my sister also come, would both be Americans in Spain, though so divided in our feelings about ourselves at home. For of course people my age and of my background in Tampa always say "they" when we talk about Americans.

That feeling persisted for a few days: I came to believe that it had something to do with the rain, for not until it stopped in Infiesto, a small town in Asturias, did I find myself with Spaniards to whom this background of mine was natural and close to their experience. We had finally taken the bus from Irun which follows the Cantabrian coast, a twisting, high ride above the rocks and turbulent October seas, until it turns inland in Asturias; and we got off at Infiesto near Oviedo, the capital of the province, to see the place where my brother-in-law had lived as a young man. We arrived the night of Saint Teresa's day, the patron saint of Infiesto, and the annual fiesta was going on. Or what was left of it, for the rain had ruined most of the activities and the town had no dance halls or auditorium to which people could retire. Nevertheless, the one hotel with heat was booked solid, and we walked in a fine drizzle to the other hotel of Infiesto, called the Gran Hotel though it had no heat, running water or any of the comforts to entitle it to the name.

But we were in Asturias and the accent and manners of everyone we met were home to me. I didn't hesitate, consequently, to tell the hotel manager—he was also the bartender downstairs—what I was doing in Spain, and he told me he had an uncle in America, in a very fine pueblo called Scarsdale. "Miamán, Miamán?" he said, trying out

14

the sound of the name. "No, I have not heard of it, but then I have never been in Galicia. So you are the son of a Gallego! Well, there are dozens of aldeas around Infiesto too, each with its own name, and I am certain they do not appear in any maps. You have looked in the maps?"

I said yes and he gave me that look which meant that it was an honor for him to be talking to a man who had maps and the intelligence to read them. There was a pause in the rain and we decided to go out, though it was eleven, to look at the fiesta. "With your permission," he said, "I shall introduce you to a company of musicians from Galicia who are staying here. Their job is about done and they will be coming back before they leave on their bus. If you do not stay out too long, you can meet them and find out."

He ran to the door when we started out. "Stay out and enjoy the fiesta," he called. "Do not worry about coming back soon. Enjoy yourselves and I shall ask them myself about Miamán!"

I knew we were at the far end of town and right across from the railroad station, but we could tell none of that by looking, just that the street sloped down through the dark toward the center of town where there were lights and noise. In the plaza, strings of colored lights were strung from tree to tree, and across from it, in what looked like a large empty lot between buildings, there was a stand for an orchestra. Everything was wet and there were puddles everywhere, but as soon as the drizzle stopped, a three-man band boosted by a bagpipe began playing *pasodobles,* and in a moment it was like the Centro Asturiano in

Tampa with couples doing the two-step in straight, marching lines and the old women sitting in folding chairs along the edge of the lot. Further down the main street there were stands like those at any fair in the world, roulette games, barkers trying to catch the attention of passers-by; the difference in Infiesto being that it was no problem to catch the attention of anyone: they stopped, listened, giggled, but only rarely pushed forward and placed a coin on the counter. I wore a beret and we did not stick out too much, but occasionally a group would notice us and they would look at us without any attempt to hide their interest.

"Why don't you talk to them?" my wife would say and my son would echo her. But I had become very shy, and the rain and long day were an excuse to go back to the Gran Hotel, for the dancing had to stop in the square and there was nothing else to watch.

As soon as we walked into the little bar of the hotel—I meant to ask for a key to our room but I stopped myself in time for I suddenly realized that one didn't exist and, in any case, served no purpose—the manager came out from behind the counter and led me to the dining room. "One of the musicians has heard of your father's aldea," he said, and pointed to a table where a half-dozen men were busy eating.

They looked like workers, not show business, but they all wore shiny red jackets and they all got up at once as I approached, as for an impresario. After we shook hands and told our names to one another, the one standing at the

head of the table said, "You may rest assured that Miamán exists. I have heard speak of it."

"You have not been there yourself?"

"No, but I have heard of it." He looked at my face and
saw I was disappointed that he had not been in Miamán
himself. "It is near Santiago de Compostela, which is
where I come from."

"Oh," I said, and I thought about the address my
mother had given me; it listed Ordenes, another city in
the province of La Coruña, as the city nearest to Miamán.

"Yes, you will have no trouble," the musician said.

"It is not on any of the maps," I said.

"Miamán, that is the name?" he said, and I nodded. "I
have heard speak of it."

"You are an American?" one of the others asked; it burst
out of him.

"But the son of a Spaniard!" said the Asturian manager.
And it made them all laugh with pride.

Upstairs in our room, the knowledge that my father's
home town still existed—if those Galicians were not just
being amiable and telling me what I wanted to hear—was
not enough to warm us. We had begun to catch sore
throats from the days of rain and the chill of Infiesto, and
our stomachs were not right. We could not take a bath
and warm up, we could not sit and talk, we could not read
even directly under the forty-watt bulb hanging from the
ceiling; we could only get into those old, lumpy beds and
pull the covers over us. They were a surprise: the coarse

linens, the quilts, the mattress stuffing—was it straw? —were like a balm, and we called out to one another in the pitch dark, having discovered this independently and all at once.

The morning was gray and a fine misty rain hung in the air and, looking out our one window, we saw an old man on a donkey approaching the little station across the road. Before we went down to breakfast, we decided to spend no more than a half a day in Infiesto, after visiting my brother-in-law's town and delivering his gift to an old friend: we would leave this cold and damp land for next summer. In the dark dining room, a girl with arms and legs red with chilblain served coffee, bread and marmalade on the cold oilcloth-covered table, and the sight of her in her thin dress made us shiver. There was no one else there, and the light, or lack of it, made it seem predawn until we noticed empty cups and crumbs on the other tables.

After coffee, we lost somewhat our hunched look, but it was still gray and the rain continued. The manager caught us looking out the front door at the donkey, and said, "Well, the fiesta is over, all we have ahead of us is the winter." And he laughed because he did not really mean it. "I spoke to the man with the taxi and he will be here soon. There is a problem, he can only be with you until lunch. He has to take the Fernandezes to a funeral in Oviedo."

"Oh, that's all right," I said.

"I assured him it would be," he said, and I could see he

was proud to be our manager. I told him the girl who served us coffee had said there was a train in the early afternoon for Oviedo and that we meant to take it, and his face showed his disappointment. "The sun will be out today," he said. "This rain is about over."

I explained to him that we only had three days to get to Barcelona to meet a friend, that we wanted to spend a day in Oviedo before returning to Irun where we had left our bags, and that, in any case, we would be returning in the spring or summer. "Well, in that case . . ." he said approvingly. During the next year I often explained our plans in the most intimate detail to people we had just met; even when, as now, I was leaving out one detail—our discomfort—to soothe their local pride. In Barcelona, you explained a trip to Madrid as an absolute necessity; leaving Andalusia for the north as a matter of business; and, eventually, leaving Spain as an emergency. It was the only way to respond in kind.

"And of course you must see Oviedo," the manager added, to convince himself. "It is the capital of Asturias."

He was right about the rain: we had no sooner driven past the last house in Infiesto than the sun came out. Those pitch-black vistas beyond the lighted main street last night were hills leading to mountains; Infiesto lay in a farming valley and it glistened with wet trees and bright green fields. The taxi driver was not sure where Llames, my brother-in-law's town was; he had once courted a girl from there—"But that was a long time ago, as you can see," he said, turning to smile back at us and not bothering with the road, for it was not likely that another car would show up on it. And so, of course, I told him where I was from and what I was doing in Infiesto.

"More and more people come to Infiesto now," he said. "For two summers now a painter from Holland comes with his wife. They stay at the Hotel Tamanaco and he goes out with his little car and paints pictures of the scenery. He says it is very beautiful."

He stopped at a dirt road which intersected the highway, the only one for miles, and talked to some men. "I guess I did not entirely forget," he said, and turned into the road, which started to climb up the mountain.

It was beautiful. The road along the side of the low mountain was mud and pebbles, navigable only on foot in winter, said the driver, and soon the valley was a faraway view. We found my brother-in-law's little village and the house of Señor Alas, an old friend who looked after the rent from the farm my brother-in-law still owned there. A man on the dirt road pointed up the hill to a large house when we asked for Señor Alas, and we got out of the taxi —the driver, of course, got out and followed too—and walked up the lane to the house. Señor Alas turned out to be an old man standing in the field nearest the house; he held a long staff which he used to keep cows away from the corner of the field which ended in a steep declivity. "You came for Saint Teresa's fiesta?" Señor Alas said, and we of course said yes.

Señor Alas wore wooden shoes, but we jumped from stone to stone to reach his house. It stood on the highest point of the hill and was large and comfortable like any

American farmhouse. The only difference was the entrance: it was simply a door stuck into one side of the house with two bare cement steps leading to it. They knew we were coming and we were no surprise to his wife when she met us inside. To them it was quite natural that we should be in Llames, and they led us to the *galería*, an enclosed porch surrounded with windows, and we talked. This was the way I had thought Spain would be, a coming home.

Señor Alas had lived in Tampa from 1904 to 1909 and then he left it for New York, where he met his wife. They moved from there to Quebec before they returned to Asturias at the end of the first world war. His wife laughed: "I used to speak a little French, better than the English I learned in New York, but now I have forgotten them both." Out the window you could see scattered farmhouses, patches of open fields, thick trees, sloping hills in the foreground, and mountains across the valley. From this village on the side of the mountain, a group of some twenty houses around a tavern, had come at least twenty-five people I knew in Tampa. And their descendants now numbered a couple of hundreds.

The children we had seen in the yard were the Alas' grandchildren, and a woman who appeared under one of the windows was their daughter. "She still speaks some French," her mother said when she came inside to join us. The daughter brought in a pink-cheeked, gray-haired old man. He had heard that a taxi driver had been asking directions for the Alas' house and decided it must be the visitors from Tampa. He was the brother-in-law of an in-law of a cousin of mine, and he too had been warned of our coming. "The letter said you left on the first of last month and I had thought, since it is now the fifteenth, that you had not left after all." He was puzzled when I told him I had not taken a Spanish ship which would have left me in Asturias but had, instead, gone to Paris first.

Yes, Señor Alas confirmed, they had all heard of our coming, and my brother-in-law had sent him a power of attorney so that when I arrived Señor Alas could take me to the bank and give me five hundred dollars from his account, accumulated rent from the farmhouse that Señor Alas managed for him. "He wants you spend it while you are in Spain, for he says he does not expect to be able to come here ever and do so himself," he explained. "Is that true?"

I said I could not understand how Pepin, my brother-in-law, could stay away from so beautiful a place.

Señora Alas pointed out the window. "There is El Palacio. You can see it from here."

"A palace?" I said; there was a long, high stone house surrounded by cultivated fields. "Is that a palace?"

"That is Pepin's farmhouse," Señor Alas explained. "We call it El Palacio. It has always been called that because it is the largest house in Llames. And it has the best farmland."

My wife and son and I stood by the window and looked at that stone house and thought what a magnificent summer place it would make; but we did not say it. "What a wonderful place to live," my wife said, instead.

Señor Alas explained very seriously that the house

22

would really have to be entirely rebuilt. "And it is a pity that Pepin does not come and make use of the place. The tenant farmer pays not quite one hundred dollars a year rent and the taxes take one fourth of that." I figured that five hundred dollars was about seven years' income. "I have been trying to sell it for him but there are not many people even asking."

When Señor Alas found out that we were taking the afternoon train to Oviedo, there was a shocked pause. I explained, as I had to the manager of the hotel, and they agreed and explained to one another why I was being sensible in waiting until summer to return. But it meant we immediately had to go to the bank in the town of Arriondas, and Señor Alas went inside to dress in something more suitable than what he was wearing for tending cows.

"Arriondas!" I said, and remembered an old story of Pepin's.

Pepin had been born in Tampa but he came to visit Llames with his mother when he was nineteen, after his father died. The civil war broke out while they were there, and as Franco's army neared their valley they began to think of going back to Tampa. When he heard that the American consulate in Gijon announced that an American warship would be coming to pick up American citizens, he walked the fifty miles to Gijon, and there found out that he could leave on it but could not take his mother because she was not an American citizen. Pepin told the consul that he would stay, and the consul gave him one piece of advice: "Do not take sides. Stay out of trouble and have your birth certificate with you at all times."

In Asturias the Republicans fought with their backs to the sea; the Basque provinces on the Atlantic had already fallen and there was no walking to the French border; you stayed and took your chances or went up into the mountains with the guerrillas. One good friend of Pepin's, the Republican mayor of Arriondas, could do neither; he was too old for the rigors of the mountains and as the Republican mayor he was sure to be executed. He had been one of those who had lived in Tampa and worked in the cigar factories and had come back to the valley in late middle age, like most Spanish immigrants never having bothered to become a naturalized American citizen. But he had once voted in one of Tampa's crooked elections to do a friend a favor and he had been issued a voting registration card by friends of his friend on the election board. And it was this fake paper, kept as a souvenir, which saved his life: Pepin walked again to Gijon with him and left him there to wait for the ship. "So you see," we used to say, as if we had put one over on the Americans, "those crooked elections were of some use after all."

Without wooden shoes and in his Sunday clothes, Señor Alas was indistinguishable from any middle-class man in town, and I saw this immediately from the respectful manner in which the taxi driver said, "Yes, Don Leopoldo," to his instructions to take us to Arriondas. Yet it was not the clothes alone; I realized now that the driver had stayed out in the farmyard throughout the visit.

As we walked down the sloping path to the dirt road

where the taxi was parked, I apologized to Señor Alas for taking him away from his work. He would not hear of it, of course, but as he talked about conditions in the countryside, I learned that farming was now more difficult than it had been in the bad years in Spain. It was almost impossible to find any agricultural workers; they were all going to France and Belgium and Germany for jobs. "We are having to do all the work by ourselves and it is too much for us."

The bank in Arriondas was a tiny place; there were no more than three men on the whole staff, and they all came forward to greet Don Leopoldo. He explained who I was and I shook hands with each; I enjoyed that, surmising that no doubt that was also the way to behave in a small-town bank in the States, but I was to find out that in Barcelona, where the banks can be huge and modern like New York's, the same handshaking takes place. Two of the men chatted with us while the third completed some forms and gathered thirty one-thousand-peseta notes, which are the equivalent of five hundred dollars. He placed them in a neat pile in front of me and, pointing to the bottom line on the forms and handing me a pen, he said graciously, "Don Jose, this is where you sign."

I had to suppress a smile, and I was glad I did so, for the man looked, as our eyes met, completely sincere. I wondered what would happen if I explained that I was just a cigarmaker's son, a Gallego's at that, not a country burgher entitled to the "Don" from his social inferiors. But Señor Alas, who was Don Leopoldo to them, would have been shocked, and as I pocketed the pesetas and was addressed as Don Jose by each as we again shook hands, the title seemed to give me stature and solidity. The taxi driver held open the door of the car as we came out of the bank, and a little child in the street looked up wide-eyed at Don Leopoldo and me and then at my wife and son in the car.

When we dropped Señor Alas at his home, I told him that I would be sending him my address as we traveled through Spain, so that if he should visit those places, we would be sure to meet. He looked at me as if I were making a joke, as if he had never left Llames for Tampa or married in New York or started his family in Quebec. "Remember," he said, "that you have a home in this corner of Spain and that it is very beautiful in summer."

In Oviedo, we took the bus back to Irun and this time, a little more familiar with the scenery, we watched the other passengers. Everyone brought a great deal of food with them though the distances they were traveling were often quite short, and at every bus station there were long and tearful farewells. We had never seen farewells like that: entire families stood alongside the bus after it closed its doors, the women with big handkerchiefs to sop the tears as they fell, the men looking resolutely away, flushed with the effort not to cry. I told my wife that these were typical Asturians, a sweet and demonstrative people; it would not be this way in the big cities where we were going to spend the next few months, nor in Galicia where my father was born; Galicians are known to be stolid, reserved, and—well, Galicians, like those Jews from Galicia in Poland, a hardheaded, backward, crafty people

26

about whom New York Jews always made jokes, though not so much any more because the Jews of Galicia were wiped out by the Nazis.

I was wrong about those scenes. Everywhere in Spain people were in movement, going to the cities, to Germany, coming home for holidays; always with a wrench, with desperate eagerness and fear to try their fortunes; hanging out the windows of trains as they returned home, calling out to friends, searching for families on the platforms. The young, lower-middle-class matron sitting in front of us on the bus was a harbinger. She looked sad, and I thought for a while she was carsick like the others who had eaten too much. She was first going all the way to Irun, on the border of France, and the elderly gentleman who sat next to her spoke to her very kindly. When he got off, he said to her, "Everything is going to be all right. Take your trip with greater calm, and you will see that all problems will resolve themselves."

As soon as he left the bus, an older woman across the aisle changed to the seat next to the young matron. The older woman had a teased hairdo, and she wore diamond earrings and a diamond pin and several rings. She had been talking to the conductor and the driver until now— about whether airplanes are preferable to trains and buses better than cars—and now she turned her attention to the sad young matron. "You will see that you will like Paris," she began. "Though not at first, perhaps."

The young matron shook her head.

"They have strong winters there and other ways," the older woman continued. "But do not worry about the lan-

guage. Signs will do at first and they will learn to understand your Spanish."

"Oh, I have my baccalaureate," the young matron said,
"and there are French words here and there that I have at
my command. But if I do not like Paris, I will not stay.
That is what I have written my husband."

"But do not be precipitate. You will find things to do in
Paris just as anywhere. And if things are more expensive,
still, you will not live the same. You will not need the
same help. Take the apartment you will live in—a kitchen,
one living room, two bedrooms! gone are the days of big
houses. What do you think the new apartments in Madrid
are like?—a kitchen, a living room, two bedrooms, maybe
a dining room!"

"If I do not like it, I shall not stay," the younger woman
answered. "Of course, we were used during the summer to
go up to Ribadesella and enjoy ourselves at the seashore,
but true, in winter you sometimes could not stir."

"Oh yes, you will find things to do in Paris."

The young matron sighed and thought it over. "Still, if I
do not like it, I will not stay."

But about Galicians it took a while to find out how
wrong I was, for myths die hard and Spaniards, despite
their moving around, have not changed their beliefs about
those who do not come from their province or about foreigners. In Irun, the girl at the desk asked if we had been
away to see the caves of Altamira, and, now that I was used
to embarking on my autobiography with every Spaniard, I
said, among other things, that my father came from Galicia. "A Gallego!" she said and could not entirely suppress

a smile. And the Catalan manager of our apartment house
in Barcelona simply pealed off a hearty laugh at the idea
that the tall American should turn out to be the son of a
Galician. It hurt me a little, just a little; like a very faint
echo of my surprised discovery at the age of eight that to
the Americans in Tampa, those who were neither Spanish
nor Cuban nor Sicilian, I was a "Cuban nigger."

Sometimes I happily reminded myself that Franco is a
Galician and so are many of his cabinet ministers, and
perhaps that was one cause for the laughter. In time, I
found out something else: the poor seldom talk badly
about the people of other provinces, and hotel desk clerks
and apartment house managers in Spain do not belong to
the working class. In time, too, I could pronounce my c's
and z's like any Spaniard, and on my second trip to Madrid that winter I was not asked for my passport at the
hotel desk but for my identity card. Mine was a three-
months transformation and I felt very much at home in
Spain; only my clothes gave me away in the small towns.
For months I did not think about Galicia, and was not reminded of it until we counted up our money in Cadiz one
day in mid-April and decided for that and other reasons to
return to the States at the end of June. I remembered then
my resolve to look up my father's home town and return
with photographs to show my family.

We were sitting in the Plaza San Juan in Cadiz, a place
whose enchantment sounds corny when described: for ex-
ample, the bells on the clock tower of the city hall play
the theme of De Falla's "Fire Music," working up from
the opening measures on the first quarter hour to the en-

tire melody on the hour. On two sides of the plaza are a series of cafes with more sitting room on the sidewalk than inside, and we came to our favorite one every afternoon for a couple of hours to drink coffee and watch people go by. Across from our special table was the taxi stand, and the drivers and shoeshine men congregated near us and talked, the taxi drivers dashing off occasionally to take care of a client but the shoeshine men drawing their customers into the conversation going on. Cadiz is a port city and, as in all port cities, you sometimes see a drunk near the waterfront; so it was not a shock that a man was slumped over one of the tables of the cafe contiguous with ours—a cafe whose front contained enough signs in English and French to show it was trying to appeal to tourists; its bar too was a free-form shape and made of Formica, not wood—but seeing a man drunk was unusual. "I've noticed that it's always a foreign seaman who gets drunk," my wife said.

One of the waiters went over to the drunk and tried to talk to him. The man looked up and smiled wryly at the waiter and slumped again; he was Spanish. After a couple of minutes, the waiter tried again. This time the man became aroused enough to talk; he asked the waiter to sit down and have a drink with him. The next attempt was by two waiters: could they help him, they wanted to know, and offered to take him wherever he needed to go. But the man only wanted them to sit with him and have a drink. Finally, the manager of the bar, who had kept aloof from the drunk, sent one of the waiters across the street to tell a cop. The taxi drivers, the shoeshine men and we watched the waiter walk diffidently away, not liking his job, and it was perhaps because of him that the cop came over without the angry, apprehensive look of a cop with a problem.

As the cop neared the table, another showed up out of nowhere and the two talked to the drunk. It took the drunk a moment to realize they were cops and he first looked scared, but then he smiled and asked them to sit and have a drink too. We were all worried: Oh they're going to be terrible; No, see, they're just talking to him. Finally, they talked him into getting up and they stood on either side of him to cross the street; then, when we had all decided the drunk had been nicely handled, one of the cops twisted his arm and held it pinned to his back; the drunk winced but he kept on walking.

"Sons of filthy bitches!" exclaimed one of the shoeshine men. "They do not think to call the cops for one of their drunken tourists. But a poor Gallego off a ship, that is another matter. He was harming no one, the poor Gallego."

A Galician! On the other side of the plaza, the cops let him go and he walked head down, watching his feet, toward the port. I remembered that when my father got over the first attack of his illness he dragged one foot and stumbled along with an effort. We had decided to return to the States from Vigo, the port in Galicia from which my father had left and to which he returned with a limp, and that lonely drunk transformed all my nostalgia for Spain into a longing to be in Galicia, the place no one thinks of when they speak of Spain.

I tried to find an answer for that on the train taking us

there—defensively, the way Middle Westerners speak up for their home town in New York—and I decided it was because the Galicians had never found a way to make their poverty, which rivals Andalusia's, attractive and colorful. We took an overnight train to Madrid and from there another overnight train to Vigo. I tried to steel myself for our first look at its poverty, its out-of-the-way existence, and when I woke in our compartment in the morning, I closed my eyes for a moment in the moving train before drawing up the blind. I pulled it up, and right across from me stood a peasant woman carrying an enormous load of newly cut grass on her head, behind her a low house of weathered stone, and vineyards all around dancing with their stately *port de bras* down the terraced slopes to the Rio Miño. The woman looked directly at me and was gone, and all around it was green, lushly green, and the morning sun bounced off the steel-gray river, rushing over the rocks and turning silver, a full, active river which filled its bed, unlike the trickling rivers of Castile. Aiee, aiee, Galicia! No one had told me it was beautiful.

2

This first view from the train was the province of Orense, the only one of Galicia's four provinces which is landbound. The others, Pontevedra, La Coruña, Lugo, stretching north of Portugal in that order along the Atlantic, are in unending communion with the sea: even on the crudest maps their coastline never settles down to a level confrontation with the Atlantic but looks like a cardiogram whose excited peaks are the *rías*, fjords, which reach inland for miles along the valleys. Vigo sits on hills rising from one of the most beautiful of these rias and looks down on an enormous bay kept placid by the islands which almost seal it off at its mouth from the Atlantic. We planned to leave from Vigo for the States, just as thousands of Galicians have shipped for all parts of the world but mainly for the Americas. Vigo is also where they return, and it was not until we were there one whole day that I remembered a Cuban rumba we used to sing when we were kids and whose opening lines—*Para Vigo me voy/Mi negra, dime adiós!*—were all I could remember: *I'm off to Vigo/ Say goodbye to me, my black girl!* Some did return with money, and there is a town near Vigo full of prosperous chalets built by Galicians who made good in the Americas.

We stayed in a hotel in the lower city, a block from the water, and walked along the bay or up the hills into the city, marveling at the views, the busy port, the shopping district, the well-dressed people sitting in the cafes. Deep within me was lodged the knowledge of Galicia's poverty, and I felt foolish, childish, that Vigo should turn out to be both old and modern, relaxed and bustling. How could those poor, backward Galicians have built a city?

That first day we picked up our mail at a travel agency where they were so courteous that, when we asked about booking passage for the States with them, they gave us the address of the shipping line's office in the city, and explained that by dealing with them directly we would get better accommodations; they seemed not to have given any thought to their lost commission. We went over to the shipping line, booked passage and walked out again and looked at the bay: we had one month for Galicia and not much money. Enough to live well in Spain, however, and we passed up the jazzier cafe on the Calle del Principe and selected the more staid cafe at its end, one whose sidewalk tables faced a triangular plaza where the wooden trolleys of Vigo all made a turn, either to swing down toward the bay or up the commercial street into the hills.

We sat at a sidewalk table and looked down the streets to the bay, full of fishing and sailing boats, and across it to the green hills of the other shore. The people walking by that afternoon all seemed well dressed, not as outgoing as the Andalusians but happy. At our cafe the middle-class wives brought their children to meet their fathers for afternoon coffee, and behind us the ceiling-to-knee-level windows showed that it was a solid, early-century cafe: large, high-ceilinged, with mahogany wall paneling, a place you could spend the whole afternoon with a cup of coffee, where the waiters, after one day, became confidants. From the sidewalk you could not look at the sparkling bay and feel, like Rosalía de Castro, Galicia's great poet of the nineteenth century, *They look at the sea/ With sadness/ Who must look for bread/ In other lands*. Not while a rosy glass of bitter Cinzano and a plate of tiny clams sit on the table before you.

"You like Vigo?" I said to my wife and son.

She laughed and he said, paraphrasing his grandmother's letter, "It is the land of your father, how could we not like it?"

We decided to make Vigo our headquarters for the remaining month; like Cadiz, it was a city you wanted to walk in, and when you didn't, it had a cafe where you felt at home and the city walked by. My wife and son went back to the hotel to decide which bags were to be stored away until we were ready to board ship and which to take with us for our trip to Santiago and La Coruña. Like a good Spanish husband, I stayed at the cafe and went inside to watch the bullfight from Madrid on TV.

The TV sat up near the ceiling at the front of the cafe, so that the patrons at the little marble-top tables could either look out the open front to the sidewalk or up at the TV. Afternoons when there are bullfights the cafes all over Spain get filled just a few minutes before the corrida begins. I was joined at mine by a middle-aged man who said, after I had given him all the necessary and minimum assurances that it would be a pleasure to share the table with him, "Even at the cafes El Cordobes sells out every seat."

"Yes, that is something I do not think the boy is given sufficient credit for doing," I said, quoting an Andalusian fan of El Cordobes' I had talked to in Jerez. "Look at the worth he has given bullfighting. Tickets used to go begging until he came along."

"Yes, that has to be said," said the man hesitantly, then looked at me with a smile and added, "You must be an enthusiast of his?"

This was a delicate moment.

"The boy is valiant," the man said, as if urging me to come out with it.

"I have to admit that I admire him," I said, remembering that a good argument about bullfighting never imperils a relationship in Spain. And we were off: Wasn't El Cordobes just a poor, hungry gypsy boy who would do anything for money? Valiant he was, but was it not obvious that he could not *torear*—that is, do the steps or the capework as tradition demands—and as for valor, had I not noticed that often El Cordobes threw out his belly only after the horns had gone by?

I said I knew that El Cordobes was not a bullfighter in the old tradition, that he was first of all a performer—

"Aha! That is what he is—a performer!"

and that he was challenging all the ideas that people had about bullfighting. He could do a pass, any pass, as beautifully as anyone, but he chose not to do it in order to do something braver—

"What a way to dominate the bull—to smack him on the snout with the sword!"

because he wants to show people that doing a pretty pass with a bull when you know he is safe is something anyone can do. I also wanted to say that El Cordobes in the ring infuriated oldtimers the way young Marlon Brando outraged critics who wanted to see only surface technique, but I did not think my table companion had a frame of reference for that. So I hesitated and the bullfight on TV began.

El Cordobes gave one of his electrifying performances, with half the Madrid audience against him and most of the one in the Vigo cafe. He got knocked down twice by the bull during the *quites,* but with the muleta he got his own back: he kept bringing the bull to a stop and then going back for more passes. "Enough, enough!" the man with me yelled with grudging admiration. "Do not expose yourself any more, Manolo, you have done enough!" When El Cordobes went to the barrier to get his sword for the kill, a spectator, an *espontáneo,* leaped into the arena with his own muleta and managed to do three adequate passes with the bull before El Cordobes' peons got the bull away from him. The crowd applauded the espontaneo as he walked to the barrier, and he proudly took a bow; then he prostrated himself on the ground before El Cordobes, asking pardon for having worked his bull: a dangerous incident for El Cordobes, since an overworked bull is as treacherous as one which has not been studied for his idiosyncrasies. El Cordobes picked the espontaneo off the ground and patted his cheek and put an arm around him, remembering, no doubt, the times he had done this before he got his first booking. Then he went in and again got battered by the bull, but with an injured right hand he did a beautiful kill.

"You must admit," I said to my table companion, "that he deserves more applause than he gets."

"Well, man, it is only the youngsters, the women and the foreigners who like that sort of thing," he said. "If the television could get up close you would see that all those people waving handkerchiefs are foreigners!"

I told him I was a foreigner. "But aren't all Galicians foreigners, more or less, when it comes to bullfighting? Vigo does not have a bullring."

"An Americano!" He forgave me everything. "That explains it!" He called the waiter over and ordered another cognac for us both. "No, television has made all of us aficionados. True, Vigo does not have an arena, but La Coruña always did and people of a certain class always went up there for the corridas. Not now, but later in the summer. Still, it was television that made everyone an aficionado, even in Galicia."

I said I had not known that.

"Oh yes, La Coruña has everything Madrid has," he

said. "On a smaller scale, of course. But it is only two or three hours away and we go up there to enjoy ourselves." And then he recited a rhyme to characterize the cities of Galicia:

> Vigo para trabajar,
> Pontevedra para dormirse,
> Santiago para orar,
> ¡La Coruña para divertirse!
>
> (Vigo for work,
> Pontevedra for sleep,
> Santiago for prayer,
> La Coruña for fun!)

La Coruña is the northernmost of these four cities, and it seemed logical to travel straight up to it and then slowly come back down to Vigo; but when we were ready a few days later and I had taken out the photostat of my father's baptismal papers and the last letter from the old woman, I decided that I didn't want to wait any longer to see my father's home town. Santiago de Compostela is half the way from Vigo to La Coruña, three hours by train, and that would make a long enough trip for one day; we could spend a couple of days in Santiago the first time, just to look around, and then stop again on the way back from La Coruña. In two visits we would be sure to forget nothing that I would want to pass on to my mother and sister.

We never found out if Pontevedra was really a sleepy city; we went through it twice and it did look quiet and relaxed, but it was early morning once and siesta hour the next time and that may have been the reason. But La

Coruña is a swinging town, with a *paseo* time to rival any city's in Spain. And Santiago de Compostela is a city for prayer, of such intensity, however, that it does not require faith to fall in with it or to be overcome by the Galician *morriña*—nostalgia—and a contemplativeness which takes in all one's life. It is a city for sweet decisions, full of old stones, so immovable with its granite block paving and granite block buildings that it calls forth resolutions: after all, Santiago was built on a myth, on the belief that Saint James's decapitated body, put forth on a raft in the Holy Land, had drifted across the Mediterranean and up the Atlantic shores of the Iberian peninsula, the very edge of the world, to come to rest in this green land.

We arrived before noon, put our bags down in our room in a second-class hotel on a medieval street, and went out immediately. The sun was shining but the air was moist, a superb day; at the end of the narrow street we made a turn, looked back at the granite fronts and galerias and paving blocks, and then looked ahead and gasped: there was an enchanting plaza with a fountain full of horses' heads spouting water. Beyond it, up wide granite steps, was one entrance to the cathedral, its sides full of sculptures and bas-reliefs which seemed to beckon. We were on the way to the tourist office, but we changed our minds and went straight for the doors of the cathedral. "Damn it," my wife said, "I didn't bring anything to cover my head!" and I went in alone.

The wide, arched doors led into one of the arms of the transept of the cathedral, and ahead was an enormous mass of people who only allowed me to step a few feet inside before they began moving back excitedly. They were making way for an immense censer swinging threateningly over our heads; on the pulpit to the right of the main altar, a half block away, stood a tall fat priest singing in a mellow baritone voice, and the mass of people, all of whom seemed to be dressed in black, joined him in the hymn. Billows of incense floated down to us from the censer as it swung across the block-long transept and gained altitude in time to the music. The censer was some three or four feet tall and was tied to a thick rope which reached all the way up—some five stories high—to the cupola above the main altar; the rope came down again in front of the altar in many strands, all tied to a ring of wood some five feet in diameter; six men in deep red robes held on to this wide ring, turning and rising with it. They seemed to be commanded by the ring, not operating the swinging of the censer, for their feet rose off the ground and they twirled with the ring like puppets. We stood out of the censer's way, pressed against the columns of the transept, and watched it swing down from the other end of the transept, almost sweep the floor in front of the altar and, emitting flames in its rush, climb over our heads to the ceiling as the hymn reached its climax:

> Firm and sure like that staff
> Which Jesus' Mother gave to you,
> Will Spain be in the Holy Christian Faith,
> The heavenly Good you willed to us.

When the censer seemed about to strike against the ceiling, it buckled for a moment—and all of us gasped—and then started on its last downward swing, slowly, in time to its measured last verse: *Defend your beloved disciple/ Protect your nation/ Protect your nation.* And everyone rushed into the middle of the transept again to see the censer untied by the red-robed men; they put a long pole through the ring at the top, and two of them swung the ends of the pole to their shoulders and walked off with the smoking censer, making a scene like a Breughel painting.

The mass of people, now chattering and smiling and pushing, carried me out again, and I found my wife and son studying the façade of the cathedral. "What a great show you've missed!" I exclaimed, and the people around me, hearing English, looked at me and smiled, taking my enthusiasm to be like theirs. They were ruddy-faced, small people; the men wore black suits and clean white shirts neatly buttoned at the collar, but seldom a tie; the women, black dresses with a black silk apron and a black silk kerchief on their heads. They were pilgrims, of course, for this was a holy year for Santiago, since the day of the Apóstol fell on a Sunday, and they had just heard a special mass: only on such occasions during Holy Year and for important religious festivals is the censer—the *botafumeiro*—brought out and the Hymn to Santiago sung. And in the faces of the people around me I could see this honorific fact reflected.

It was marvelous to stand on the steps above the fountain, surrounded by happy pilgrims, all as astonished by the façade of ancient buildings as we. Since my wife had no head covering—and being Jewish she was very careful

about the feelings of Catholics—we had to content ourselves with the outside of the cathedral. It was too much
to take in at one look: four plazas surrounded it, and although we did not stop to study the ornamentation or the
buildings which faced the cathedral, circling it was a long
walk, full of surprising turns and grand vistas. The most
astonishing was the Plaza del Obradoiro, on which the
main entrance to the cathedral gives: an enormous square
paved in the same huge granite blocks as the rest of the
old city. At the far end from which we entered stood a low
Renaissance palace, the Hostal de los Reyes Católicos, a
government tourist hotel now; we had read about it and
knew that it was for many years the only hospital in Santiago. That fabulous place, I thought, is where my father
once stayed.

Before we entered the tourist office, I took out my father's baptismal papers and the address to which my
mother used to write many years ago. I got the first sen-
tence ready of the story that I was to tell so often in the
next twenty-four hours that Rafael, my son, learned to im-
itate me in a weary, singsong manner.

"My father," I said to the man who hurriedly got up
from an easy chair and wished me good day, "was born in
Galicia, in the province of La Coruña."

"Ah!" he said, delighted.

"In the town of Miamán." And his eyes went blank. "I
would like to visit it," I said, and read off the full address
to him: "Miamán, Ayuntamiento de Trazo, Ordenes, La
Coruña."

"You have come to the right place, for if we do not

43

know . . ." And he went behind the counter and called to a man at the farthest end to ask where the book of the province was. "First we have to find out if it exists. . . . So you are an American!"

The man at the other end came over. "But you speak Spanish so well."

"His father was born here," the other informed him.

"A Gallego!"

The first one brought out an enormous volume from under the counter and began to turn the pages.

"I have not found it on any map," I said.

"Oh, there are thousands of aldeas you cannot find on any map," he said.

"Except ours," the second man said.

"First we have to find out if it exists," the first insisted, and ran his finger down the page. "Here it is! Miamán. It has eight hundred people."

"Of course it exists," the second said. "You should have asked me. My grandfather came from there."

"Then you know Miamán?"

He shook his head, a little ashamed. "My grandfather went to Argentina and died there. All I know about Miamán is the name. But I can tell you it is near here somewhere."

"It has a baker, a tavernkeeper," the first called out. "Also a schoolteacher. What a marvelous book this is! It is the first time I have had occasion to use it." He beckoned me to join him, and we leaned our heads together to peer at the short paragraph in tiny type. "It exists."

"Can you tell me how I get there?" I said.

"That comes next," the man said, putting the book away. "We shall look it up on our map."

"So you want to visit your relatives in Miamán," the second said.

"No, I just want to see the town," I said. "That is, I do not have any relatives in Miamán." And I told him the story of my grandmother being the only one left thirty years ago and she of course must be dead.

"And then, people move away," he said. "Like my grandfather."

"Maybe you two are relatives," my wife said.

So the man told me his full name and I gave him mine, including all the last names in the baptismal papers. None were the same, and we laughed, almost relieved. "So many people leave Galicia for good," the man said.

They rolled out a long, wide map on the counter, and explained that it was not available commercially. It was handmade and they thought there might only be one other copy in the municipal palace. It covered La Coruña alone, and it listed even the tiniest aldea. We looked and looked around the city of Ordenes, a few miles to the north of Santiago but a long stretch of paper away. Then between Santiago and the sea: there was Miamán, sitting out in a little white area by itself, fed by none of the thin capillaries which reached out to the towns whose names were in bolder print.

"Do you have a car?" the man asked.

I shook my head.

The second one coughed. "It looks like a car would not get him there."

"Oh, there must be a road," the other insisted. "There always is."

They smiled when I spoke of staying overnight in Miamán. "It is an aldea," the first said. "There will be no place to stay, and in any case, you will see everything there is to see in an hour." He advised me to hire a taxi for the day; it would take me there, wait and bring me back.

When I explained at the hotel desk why I wanted to hire a taxi for the next day, they were delighted. "Your father came from one of our aldeas!"

I asked that the driver be at the hotel at ten, and so next morning we had time for a late breakfast. At a long table next to ours, a group of pilgrims chatted over their coffee and rolls; they were not the ruddy, excited and awed peasants we had seen yesterday at the cathedral; they were a middle-class group who had arrived last night after we returned to the hotel. Seven of them still sat at the long table: a young priest, two middle-aged men, four women, all sensibly dressed for travel. They were not unexcited, however, about the day ahead, and one of the women, to the chagrin of the priest, asked the waiter what a proper visit to the cathedral required.

The waiter, delighted, came closer and made a slight bow. "You go in by the main entrance on the Plaza del Obradoiro, you place five fingers in the base of the column on which rests the statue of Santiago, and you make your ten wishes, one of which will be granted to you. Then, on the other side of the pedestal, you strike your head—lightly!—on that of Master Mateu's—"

"Master Mateu?" asked the youngest of the women.

"The genius who made the statues of the Gloria Portico. There is a small statue of him there and it will give you serenity of spirit to touch it. They even say that his intelligence will flow into your head when you touch it. Then you go to confession, listen to mass, take communion, listen to the Hymn to Santiago, see the swinging censer, which we Gallegos call the *botafumeiro*. You go behind the altar and embrace the Apóstol—and you leave by the holy door!" He stepped back and bowed again. "All this you must do or why come to Santiago . . ."

A middle-aged woman asked, "But how do you embrace the Apóstol?"

The younger woman giggled.

The waiter told them that there is an entrance which leads up into the main altar, from which you can look down into the central nave of the cathedral. At that point you are directly behind the statue of the Apóstol and on the same level with him. "You place a hand on each shoulder of the Apóstol, you lean forward, and you have embraced him."

The two men exchanged glances, the young woman giggled again, and the other ladies smiled.

The priest said, "There are some customs which seem to me ridiculous. This embracing of the saint, to me that is ridiculous!"

"It is a custom," said the young lady.

"Yes, yes," said the other women.

The priest looked ahead.

"Of course, it is not an article of Catholic faith," said the young lady.

"No, no," said the older woman. "It is not a teaching of the Church."

"Not a teaching of the Church," repeated one of the men, as if announcing that he, for one, would embrace the Apóstol.

"It's a custom," repeated one of the women, her eyes on the priest.

"A custom of the time," said the same man, determined.

The other middle-aged man said, "When we venerate, we express ourselves and sometimes it shows up our ignorance."

The priest shook his head. "But there should be an attempt to learn more, to know what one is doing. You see people stand when El Santísimo goes by in procession, but they will drop to their knees when San Juan or San Geronimo or some favorite saint goes by. That should not be."

"It is ignorance," said one of the women, as if she had just thought of it.

The man who was going to embrace the Apóstol compressed his lips, but the other one, a smooth talker, answered the young priest. "Well, Father, true it should not be, it *is* ignorance, but it is an expression of good faith—the intention is there, it is a good one."

"Yes, yes," said the priest impatiently.

"Of course, I am not for fanaticism," the smooth one continued. "Countries where there is fanaticism are backward and . . . I mean where they worship Buddha and in Japan."

"Oh," said the priest, relieved, "I have been in villages

where they take the holy image out of church in procession and stop at the tavern to give Him a drink." Everyone laughed. "And they all end up drunk."

The waiter stepped forward again. "You see that here too," he said. "For San Separes we—they all get drunk. San Separes is the patron of drunks."

"Yes, I am not for fanaticism," said the smooth talker, dissociating himself from the waiter. "The more I have traveled the more I have come to see the reasonableness and civilized ways of our religion. Now that I have been in many more places in this world and observed other religions, the more I appreciate our Catholic religion."

"Have you been to Lourdes?" the young lady asked. The man nodded.

"Lourdes is more impressive than Rome," said the young lady.

"Oh yes," said an older woman.

"There is greater faith there," said the young lady.

"Oh, mass and communion for the sick at Lourdes," said the smooth one, "is elevating. To see all those people, some on stretchers, approach the altar is very impressive."

The priest got up and, without looking at them, said, "Well?"

"Yes, it is time to go," said the young lady eagerly, and they all got up and left the table. The man who was going to embrace the Apóstol winked at the waiter behind the priest's back.

We left on our own pilgrimage a few minutes later. The driver took a look at the map they had made for us at the tourist office, and said there were no roads off the main highway at the point they indicated. But he said we were not to worry; there was only one highway leading west from Santiago to the Atlantic, and there would be a road off the highway further on which, no doubt, would lead to Miamán. "We shall find it, do not worry," the man said, and the Dubra valley opened ahead of us, green and criss-crossed with farms, a lovely sight in the clear morning air. We probably shall not find the grave, I said to my wife, nor find anyone who can tell us stories about the old woman, but it'll be nice anyway: we can walk around in the town and maybe have lunch. In my mind, Miamán was like a town in the south, with a church on the main plaza, a little cafe facing it across the way; all very modest of course, but thoroughly delightful. A lovely way to spend the day.

But wherever I looked, the landscape did not return this image to me. There were huddled, scattered farm buildings with dark-red tiled roofs blackened by the years, and the only people we saw were black-robed women bending over rows of plants, young children lead-ing donkeys along the road. Still, it was all quite beautiful and explainable by everything I had heard from child-hood; Galician men left the women back on the farm and went to the cities or emigrated to make the money the land would not yield. Nevertheless, there were no towns, and I recalled that the big map at the tourist office had shown many towns on either side of the highway. I asked the driver if he had been to Miamán before and he said no. "But in a few more kilometers we shall ask," he said.

When he did, we had to turn back to the last group of buildings we had seen along the highway; it was up from that town—I was surprised those few buildings were called a town—that we would find Miamán, perhaps one or two kilometers away. The driver got out to ask a man coming along the road—he had suddenly materialized out of the houses—and the man looked briefly at us in the taxi and said that directly ahead we would find the road to Miamán. "Right next to the bank," he said, and I thought he was joking.

"Right there?" the driver said, pointing to a building which looked like a country store. "And we follow the road next to it?"

"Yes," said the man, and added, "On foot."

I stuck my head out the window, and the man said, "It is a road, but not for this kind of vehicle."

The driver drove the equivalent of one city block to the little building which was the bank, turned off the highway, and parked facing the road we were to take to Miamán. By the time we got out of the car, the man who had given us directions caught up with us, and he listened with interest while I told the driver that since we only planned to speak to the priest at the church and perhaps some others and to have lunch, he could count on our being back there before two thirty.

"You can come with us if you like," I said to be courteous, but the driver said he would wait for us. I thought that he showed an exceptionally fine sensibility in knowing that we would rather make this sentimental journey alone.

We moved away from the taxi and looked at the gutted dirt road climbing the hill ahead of us; before it turned out of sight, there were three or four houses on either side of it, looking as raw and unfinished as the red dirt road. There were that many women standing in the road talking, and two or three children playing; as we made our way toward them, they stared in astonishment, and it was not until we were past them that their high-pitched peasants' voices started up again. We looked at one another and I knew that if I were one of those people along the road I would have laughed out loud at the sight of us, we were that strange. And I suspected we were also foolish: what had made me talk about going to Miamán for three or four hours as if we were on a jaunt downtown to a matinee?

We looked at our shoes; they were laughable. Not that the road was muddy; it was hard-packed and dry, but it was rutted, and the stones and pieces of marble imbedded in the red earth made themselves felt through the thin soles of our city shoes. The voices of the women near the highway were soon inaudible, and around us and behind us, as the road turned, were only eucalyptus and pines: the inspiring stillness of nineteenth century poetry reigned about us and made us hesitate and whisper, as if the entire countryside could overhear us with our city rudeness. The mixed scents of pine and eucalyptus made the fresh air even fresher, and it was almost a reflex to stop and fill our lungs with it. These were the pines of the green pine forests of the poet Rosalía de Castro! No wonder my father had believed that if he could get back here he would be cured of the illness he caught in the hot, flat country of Florida, in the shut-in, airless world of the cigar factory.

Those many mountain lanes, said Rosalía, whose one trip away to Madrid left her desolate, *that to deep valleys fall . . . / There at the top the murmur of brave pines and below sweet peace./ In these heights clear light, purest breezes, rescue solitude,/ strange rumors which awaken fearless thoughts of liberty.* In Rosalía the perfume of these pines aroused "mad and strange desires," in us the eerie sense that with each stretch along the winding, climbing lane the centuries fell back. We were lost in time . . . until we came to the end of the pine forest, and there, framed by trees on either side of the lane whose branches met at the top, was a medieval landscape: the church on the highest ground across the open fields, and below it, as if escaping to the valley, the huddled houses of the farmers.

We looked at the scene, our eyes going back to the church tower after every glance, and I took out, as at the tourist office, the photostat of a statement once written by the village priest, in which he attested to the fact that in the registry of the church of San Gabriel of Miamán there exists a page on which it is written that I, Don Andres Pedroso, parish priest, have this afternoon of 28 July 1890 solemnly baptized with the name of Jose a boy born this morning at dawn, legitimate son of Jose de la Iglesia and Dolores Andeiro, natives and neighbors of this parish. This parish! There it was, preserved in sunlight and beckoning like one of those mysterious lands of the Saturday matinee movie serials of my childhood. Having navigated the dismal swamp, full of man-eating crocodiles, should the hero press forward to the jewel city? Will his adventures now be crowned with happiness or do new dangers lurk?

We took photographs, of course. That's what I had come for, to look at it for myself and to send back photographs to my mother and sister. Someday my son would show the color pictures of himself and of the group of houses beyond his shoulder, on the other side of the field of corn seedlings. We looked at the place, he would say, and talked to . . . and we did find someone who remembered. It meant a lot to the old man though he didn't show it: he said he was doing it for his sister and mother.

As soon as I put away the camera, two girls showed up on the road; they had come down a lane which descended from the pine forest and joined our climbing one just beyond the frame of trees. The girls were short and chunky and pink-cheeked and they looked at us with open curiosity. I pointed to the church up the hill and asked if it were San Gabriel. "Yes!" they said, as if asking how I knew, and before they walked ahead, showing us their reddened, chilblained legs and their heavy men's shoes, they told us the parish priest had died six months ago. "One comes over from Trazo every Sunday, but you can ask the priest's maids at the house."

They clumped ahead of us, their heads down, waiting to put more distance between us before they burst into talk about us. We hung back to give them privacy, as if that open country, the valley behind us and the hills

above, were a small crowded room. We kept our eyes on
the church steeple, the farthest building on the hill
ahead, and lost the girls at the same time that we discovered the road did not take us right up to the church. Good
city folk, we were nonplussed—how to get up to the
church one country block away? I heard the girls' voices
and tracked them to a house on the road. At first they
could not understand why I did not recognize the church
from the three or four houses on the hill, then showed us a
path to it along one of the houses; we followed it with the
uneasy feeling that we were trespassing.

The church was not only closed but looked unused, and
its stone walls were worn and blackened and weeds grew
in the cracks; where the stone met the wet ground, green
moss spread upward. Between the gate and the door,
where water had seeped mysteriously, a stone slab was
imbedded in the ground; the inscription said that here
was buried Don Andres Pedroso, priest of this parish; Don
Andres, the man who had christened my father and signed
the baptismal papers which I carried in my hand. He had
been dead thirty years, and we looked at the worn stone
and mud and wondered if we would find one like this for
my father and the old woman.

The houses across the muddy path in front of the
church looked like a series of barns; I could recognize no
front door, no place at which one could properly knock. I
decided, instead, to follow the tapping sound coming from
behind the high wall on the farther side of the church. It
led us into a cemetery, not like the church burying
grounds of New England, but a small enclosed yard in

whose high walls were burial niches. A man stood in the center of the yard chipping at a stone, and since he did not look at us, we made a round of the walls looking for my grandmother's name. There were many of my family names but either not spelled the same or combined with unknown ones, so that I could not say, yes, this is my grandmother or my aunt or my father. I turned to the man chipping at the stone, and when he looked at me, I realized he had not done so before because he was so consumed with curiosity that he had not trusted himself to keep his dignity.

He was not from Miamán, and the stone he was working on was the headstone for the grave of the priest who had died six months ago. He told us that the priest from Trazo, his own aldea, had been there this morning but had already left. "I do not recommend that you talk to the servant of the old priest if you want information," he said, with an apologetic smile. "She is an old woman and . . . you know."

I told him my story—I was to tell it three more times that day—and asked his advice about whom to talk to, who might remember my father and the old woman. He looked at me steadily and it took him a moment to reply. "So you are an American and your father came from Miamán!" he said, dropping his dignity. Finally, he told me that the house along whose side we had walked to get to the church was a tavern, and that the man there, being from Miamán, might help me. We shook hands, and as we walked out the narrow opening in the wall of the cemetery, my wife pointed to a name on one of the shiny new niches near the exit. It said "Dolores Andeiro," but that was my grandmother's maiden name, so it could not be she.

We peered through the glass top of the tavern door, and saw, dimly, that there was a counter inside. Until then we were almost certain the man had made a mistake: how could there be a tavern without a plaza or chairs sitting in the sunlight, as in all the towns of Spain? And the door was locked. Yet we could see the counter inside. So we knocked and knocked, and a middle-aged man came from an inner room and opened the door. He sold us, after we conferred about his stock, one beer and one lemon soda, neither, of course, cold.

"I am an American," I said, "and my father was born in Miamán." And that delighted look came over his face as with everyone in Galicia to whom I told the story.

He tried out my family names aloud. "Yes, there are people with such names in Miamán—"

I interrupted: "But I do not expect to find family, for my aunt and my grandmother had no relatives, and if my aunt had children their names of course would not be Andeiro or Yglesias."

"The problem is this," the middle-aged man said, "I was not born in Miamán and I have lived here only a few years.

"I come from Todoya," he added, and did not explain, for I could see that everyone knows Todoya.

"My father died in 1931 and my aunt two years later," I said, "and then there was only the old woman left."

"Such a long time ago," he said. "All that happened before I was born, so even if I had been born in Miamán I would not know."

"I should have realized," I said, and was again reminded that in Spain everyone looked at least ten years older.

"You must talk to some old people," he said. "In the first house down the hill there is an old man. His name is Eliseo Carballo and he is very old but he will remember."

He told us to go back to the church and look for a path directly across from it. It led down to the cultivated fields, and I was to ask for Eliseo Carballo at the first house in the group we had seen when we came out of the pine forest. There was a path, just as there had been one next to the church, and as we started down the sloping hill we could hear the man from Trazo chipping at the stone in the churchyard. Ahead of us were the fields of seedling corn and young wheat, and too far for us to call any greeting were women and some men bending over their work. The first we waved to did not wave back, but straightened up. Then others stood up too, and finally one waved and the others followed suit. But none came over, for they saw we kept walking. "Such tiny plots," my wife said. "It can't pay them to plant such little bits of corn."

The path came to an end at the back of the first house, at a level of three or four feet above it, and we had to climb down rough, improvised steps of stone slabs. "We're trespassing," my wife warned. "This is someone's yard."

I shrugged my shoulders and climbed down, for there were no fences; there were just spaces of trampled ground or lanes between the houses, puddled where it was not

mushy mud. From a distance all this mud and rotting tim-
ber and pitted stone had been color tones in an alluring
landscape; close up—and the climb down the stone slabs
from the green fields made us face it abruptly—it was a
frightening shock. We didn't know where to turn: again
there seemed to be no front to houses, only barnlike struc-
tures with overhangs propped up by rotting poles stuck
into the mud, and beyond them were openings into the
low buildings looking like the mouths of caves. Yet the
place did not look ramshackle, not a rickety hooverville of
ours: this was solid poverty, built to last.

I started toward the opening in the first house, but my
wife called me back; coming up a lane beyond the yard
were two girls, each leading a team of two oxen pulling
low, open wagons loaded with cuttings of a thorny bush
with a yellow flower. The wagons took all the space between the buildings, and the oxen moved forward slowly,
for although the girls carried long sticks in their hands
they did not urge the oxen with them. Oxen and girls
looked at us with wide-open eyes, and when I raised my
camera and took their picture, the girls smiled and the
older one came forward. She wore knee-high boots, kerchief, a plain dress and dangling earrings.

I told her I was looking for Señor Eliseo Carballo, and
she pointed to the first house and said he was not there
today, so I told her why I was looking for him. She was an
intelligent girl and did not allow herself to become awed
by the wonder of it, but looked down at the ground to
consider how best to help me. The younger one said something to her in such thick, unfamiliar Galician that I did

not get the sense of it, and the older one shook her head impatiently.

"Andeiro, you said?" the girl questioned me.

I explained that there were no more relatives of my grandmother's, for her only daughter had died, and in any case, the name which would have survived would not be my grandmother's maiden name. "Perhaps there is someone named Yglesias?"

First she shook her head, then she said, yes, there were people of that name but it could not be they. "Wait a minute, and let me get my mother." She went into the first house and that is how I knew she was Eliseo Carballo's granddaughter. Her mother must have been watching us, for she came out immediately; she looked like the younger girl and had the same stunned, unbelieving look. I told my story again, but her older daughter was dissatisfied with her suggestions. And we trusted the older daughter.

"I am going to take you to the house of some people named Andeiro—"

"But there should be no relative of that name," I said.

The girl nodded to show she had understood the first time. "The old man of that family is very old, even older than my grandfather. He should remember, except that he is very old."

So we followed her down the lane she had come by with the oxen, and I told her how beautiful Miamán was. "It is very ugly in winter," she said. "Even now we cannot wear proper shoes." I had seen her notice my wife's shoes as we navigated through the mud, and she kept pointing to the less muddy spots for my wife to step on. At the end of the lane, between the houses, a group of children played with a dog, and their clothes and legs and arms were covered with caked dirt. The dog crouched in the mud, a little doll between its jaws, and the girl called to one of the children to point it out to them. The children didn't seem to care, and when I looked at the dog again, I saw that the white fuzzy object in its mouth was not a doll but a young dead rabbit.

With houses and barns on either side, the lane had been dark and chill, and it was good to turn at the end of it toward an open area. This last house at the other end of the settlement was like the others—the same overhang darkened the doorway in the stone wall—but a large yard, facing south, lay in front of it in sunlight. The ground there was dry and green with grass, and in the center, dappling the yard with its branches, grew a giant apple tree; on the edges of the yard were more apple trees and cherry trees, and at one end we saw the traditional *orreo*—a charming cabin with slatted walls set high on stilts above the ground, used to store corn; beyond it the ground sloped into the farmlands in the valley.

We stopped in the shadow of the overhang, for the girl went to the doorway and called, and we saw that the house extended all the way along that side of the yard to the southern tip of the ledge over the valley, forming a kind of dark wall for the happy, open yard. Two people came to the door. First, a young adolescent boy who looked at us with large brown eyes as shy and appealing as those of the oxen; his pants and shirt were full of patches but very clean, and he was beginning to outgrow them. I thought the woman who followed him was his mother; like the peasant women we had seen she wore a black kerchief to match her dress and heavy men's shoes. With a quick look and a slight nod she took in the astonishing sight of foreigners just beyond her door; then she closed her face earnestly to listen to the girl who had brought us.

The girl stood with her back to us and spoke in Galician, so I only intermittently caught a snatch of her explanation of our presence. I interrupted to say that I hoped simply to find someone who might remember my grandmother and possibly my father, and the woman nodded sympathetically and closed her face again to think over the problem. The girl raised her head as she spoke and nodded toward the inside of the house, meaning, I thought, the old man who lived there. The woman turned to the boy and quickly gave him some instructions, and asked us in. In the moment we hesitated, the boy disappeared, and as we walked toward the doorway, the girl said she must be getting back to her house, for she felt sure the old man could help us.

The woman nodded. "Yes, yes," she said, backing into the house and motioning us to come in, though she was obviously worried about the state of the house. "My father is lying down—he has to lie down for he is short of breath—but I will tell him and he will come out."

The three of us stood in the doorway and looked in, and it was our turn not to look surprised at what we saw. Beyond us, in twilight, was a large room, high-ceilinged at the center and sloping toward the sides, so that a little

doorway at the other end was shorter than the woman.
There was no window to be seen, but a shaft of light from
a front corner, on the other side of the entrance passage,
told us there was one opening in those thick walls. A
wooden trestle table faced us immediately beyond the
passageway, and except for two long benches and three
wooden kitchen chairs which she brought out from a corner, there was no other furniture in the room. The three
chairs were, no doubt, the pride of the house, and she
placed them near the doorway where we had come to a
stop. Not until we were seated and she had explained
again that she was getting her father and that it was no
trouble—for we had, of course, demurred and said we did
not want to bother them—did she leave us.

She climbed four wooden steps in a dark corner of the
inside wall, and pushed in a door to another room of the
house. We heard her heavy shoes striking the floor before
she closed the door behind her, and realized then that this
big room we sat in had no wooden floor. It was hard-
packed earth as dark as the walls but lighter than the ceiling, which was made black by the open fire. One fourth of
the room was taken by the fire smoldering on the ground,
diagonally at the other end of the room from us; three
huge iron pots hung over it from the low ceiling, which
was shaped into a flue at that corner to draw the smoke.
Across from the fire sat one of the benches, the other
alongside the outer wall next to the fire. Above the second
bench, on a shelf, sat an old radio, as familiar an anomaly
as a television antenna on a tenement roof, and we looked
at one another and mouthed our discovery: They have

electricity! We looked for the light, and saw a bulb hanging from a wire just beyond the wooden table. Around the entrance passage, there was a corner of the room we could not see without getting up. We didn't get up; we sat quietly in our chairs and looked at the long dark room, like an audience who knows that something is about to happen, for the room was full of presences, palpably there.

The woman did not sit down when she returned; it did not occur to her to do so or to excuse herself for continuing to work, bringing kettles of water from the room beyond the little door by the fire to the corner beyond our sight at the front. Yet she did not neglect us. I had the baptismal papers out and I read her the names of the godparents of my father, and she explained that she came from Paramos, that the old man who would soon be out was her father-in-law, and that was why she could not tell me anything. Still, she said, the godmother's name was familiar: there were people named Seijas in Paramos. "And so you have come all the way from America!" she said, and brought her hands together in front of her breast and then crossed herself.

"And you have never been in Miamán before?" she asked when I went over the story of my father. No, I explained, my father had expected to return to us and we were very poor and my mother had all her family in Tampa and so we never saw him again. "*Poveriños, poveriños!*" she said, lapsing into Galician; her eyes filled with tears for my father's two young, fatherless children, and she raised her thick, rough hands to cover her mouth.

"My husband's father will know," she said, and crossed

herself again. "And the others, they will be able to tell you something."

"And this is your son?" she said, looking at Rafael and putting her head to one side, her gesture of admiration. "And the lady, your wife, she knows Spanish too?" My wife smiled and half shook her head and I said for her that she understood it but did not speak it. "Oh she will not understand us for we do not speak proper Castilian and she must pardon us because of our ignorance."

The old man came down the steps at the back of the long room carefully, taking them one at a time, and as soon as he got to the bottom, he turned his head and looked for us. But he averted his face quickly, like a bird on watch, and slowly made his way to the front doorway. We stood up to greet him and the woman said, "My father," and he said, "Carlos Andeiro Piñeiro." He had dressed completely in what were, no doubt, his Sunday clothes—the jacket did not match the pants and the many patches neither of them nor one another—and he turned to each of us, including my son, as if there were no distinctions and each one of us were an incalculable honor to find there in his home.

He had become slight with age; the skin on his face was stretched thin over the bones, and its color, a mottled silver-gray and pink, showed that his shortness of breath was caused by a cardiac condition. It took a moment to persuade him that it was all right for him to take the chair Rafael had been sitting in, and although we faced one another and our knees almost touched, he managed to look into uninhabited space from the little eyes sunk deep in his cheekbones. His eyebrows seemed perpetually raised to allow him to peer out into the world, and his eyes were a hazy blue, indeterminate as a baby's: you knew that in a short time they would take on their final hue.

With the baptismal papers in my hand, I told him the story again, and whenever I paused, he nodded and exhaled audibly. Finally, I came to the end of the story and he exhaled a longer breath and moved in his chair and made a thin sound of agreement. Then he waited. His daughter-in-law paused on her way to the fire and shook her head as if this were what she had feared.

I started to speak to fill up the silence, and the old man said, leaning forward a little as if he knew his voice hardly carried, "You said their names were . . ."

I read them from the baptismal papers although I knew them by heart. He nodded and settled back again. "And you come from Cuba?" he said, and smiled to himself.

"No, the United States of America. It is to the north of Cuba . . ." And I went over the details again and told him how my father had first emigrated there and then crossed over to Florida. When I finished the story a second time, we were silent for a long time. I looked round at my wife and son. I did not know how to get up and leave.

"Dolores Andeiro . . ." the old man said.

"That was the maiden name of my grandmother here in Miamán."

The old man smiled and nodded.

"When she married she became Dolores Yglesias," I said.

His face lost what there had been of recognition, and
we became silent again.

The woman called out to us, "He is seventy-seven years
old. Or maybe seventy-eight."

In the disappointed silence which followed again, I saw
the old man gather up his strength and take a deep
breath. "My aunt Dolores—" he began.

"Tía Dolores was Dolores Andeiro!" said the woman,
coming close, a black kettle in one hand.

"My aunt Dolores had a son and he went away to America and when he came back he was very sick . . ."

"Aiee, aiee," said his daughter-in-law, and crossed her
self with her free hand. "It is a miracle!"

3

"... but he got better and went back to America and died there . . ." The old man nodded to himself, then looked at me to see if he had pleased me.

"Oh, then he could not have been my father," I said, and got the impression, which was to stay with me for some time, that the old man had simply returned information I had given him and that he had inadvertently got it wrong. I was on my guard and I was sorry. "You say he went back to America and died there?"

Those hazy eyes would not look at me any more; he looked down at his lap and nodded, not with assurance but as if he hoped that if he looked away the nod would do.

"No! No!" someone in the doorway shrieked, and I saw a little woman who must have been standing there while the old man spoke. "You have forgotten, Tía Dolores' son

68

died in Santiago. He did not go to America, he went to the hospital in Santiago!"

She seemed to be leaning down to talk to him, though her voice was penetrating enough. Then the old man was my father's cousin, I thought, and I got up as the little woman came over to me.

"Do not leave," she said, unaware that I got up because she was a lady and the news excited me. "Carlito saw me when I was halfway here to get the midday meal and I sent him to get my mother. She is older than him—my father," she explained, nodding to the old man, "but her memory is better. She will be able to tell you."

She leaned toward me and smiled self-consciously, to apologize for having burst in on our conversation. She had large, lively brown eyes and strong white teeth, and when I introduced myself and my wife and son, she looked at us boldly and with curiosity; she did not stop leaning forward, a stance that made her seem to beg pardon for her every movement. She looked from one to the other of us under thick eyebrows which met at the bridge of her nose, and then took off the wide-brimmed straw hat she wore over the black kerchief tied under her chin—it gave her a curiously fashionable look—and asked the other woman, "Ana, would they like to drink something while they wait?"

She turned quickly to look at us again, and I realized she was on guard for the moment when we would notice that she could not straighten up, that she was hunchbacked. Her voice went soft with self-pity, and she said to her father, "Tía Dolores' son was too sick to go back to

America. He only went to Santiago to the hospital, never to America."

"Never to America?" I said, disappointed again. "You see, my father came back twice to Miamán while he was sick. The first time he went back to Cuba."

"That is where he came from—Cuba," she said, and waited for me to nod in agreement.

I didn't know what to answer her. My father's story suddenly seemed too complicated to explain, for I was afraid that she too was only repeating what I had said. I tried to remember what new information she had given me and I could not recall just what I had been saying when she got to the house.

Suddenly she burst out, "I was too young when it all happened! I know I look like a woman of a hundred, but I fell a long time ago and sustained a blow to my back and it has left me looking this way."

I heard my wife sigh, and the woman turned to her with that leaning look, like a child seeking affection.

Then she looked at her father. "But he did not die in America," she said, as if it were the old man she had to convince. "He died in Santiago. That I remember."

The woman she had called Ana crossed herself and stopped again. I got up and said, "We may all be cousins." And Ana crossed herself again, the little hunchbacked woman looked up at me at the level of my waist with startled, wide-open eyes, and the old man still looked away, a faint smile on his delicate face. "But you say your father's cousin died in a hospital, not an asylum?" I said, and the spell was broken: we were not cousins.

"My mother will remember, she is the one with the good memory," the little woman said, and I sat down again. "You see, we people in the aldea are a little foolish. We do not know as much as we should."

Again Ana said, "You will have to forgive our ignorance." But there was something in the way she said it which sounded as if she were contradicting and also asking forgiveness for her little hunchback sister-in-law.

"What is happening?" my wife whispered in English, and I answered that I didn't know. Ana and the little woman looked at one another, and decided simultaneously that it was uncomfortable for us inside the room. It was cold there, the sun shone in the yard, and the lady, my wife, would enjoy it more. We got up and they took the chairs—we were not allowed to carry them—out to the yard. Again, the sweetness of the air; illogically, mysteriously, it made me feel that, yes, perhaps these people were my cousins. How dark and confused it had been inside!

Rafael ran after a small furry puppy, and chickens scooted away from his path. A golden mound of hay stood where the sun could always reach it, and I noticed for the first time a wagon loaded high with the thorny, yellow-flowered bush we had seen growing everywhere on our walk from the highway. A thick tree trunk lay on the ground under the apple tree; a lovely place to sit, but the women worried about my fine clothes.

"No, no!" the little hunchback shrieked when I headed for it, and made me sit on the straight-back kitchen chair she had brought to the yard. And then an old woman was walking slowly toward me across the yard, taking little steps, the boy with the patched pants at her side. His big brown eyes were exactly like the little hunchback's, but he seemed to be hanging back while she always appeared to be darting forward. When they had gotten halfway across the yard, the boy went toward Rafael, but the old woman kept on toward me, chuckling as she walked, the sight of us in her yard a source of astonished delight.

She wore a black kerchief and a long dress of a tiny flowered print, and she said, "Yes, yes!" or "What, what?" to anything said to her. And when I shook her hand, she laughed out loud. "Dolores Andeiro was your aunt?" I said, and she became confused and looked to the little hunchback.

"No, no, Tía Dolores was my father's aunt," the little woman said, and pointed to her father sitting on one of the upright chairs, "but my mother remembers her." She raised her voice even louder. "You remember Aunt Dolores?"

"Yes, yes!" the old woman said, and waved a hand as if to say indubitably, "I remember her."

"And her son who went to America?" her daughter asked.

"He got sick," the old woman said. "He died in the hospital." And she chuckled, proud of her memory.

"What hospital?" I asked, and she became confused and looked at her daughter again.

"There was only one hospital," the hunchback said. "It is now the Hostal."

"Not an asylum?" I said.

"Yes, yes!" the old woman exclaimed, and looked around and chuckled.

I was disappointed and so was Ana, but the little hunchback most of all; she wanted us to be relatives and the unsatisfactory answers made her impatient, so that she could not stand still. "Here, here," she said, as if to distract me, "this is my daughter." And she pushed forward a little girl who had been one of the children playing in the muddy lane. The little four-year-old smiled; she had a pink round face, blue eyes, chestnut hair, totally unlike her mother. I looked for Carlito, the boy with the patched pants, and the little hunchback said, "He is my son," as if she knew that it was he who looked like her.

I nodded and said, "He is like you and she is like her father." And the little hunchback laughed shyly, and pushed the little girl toward where Rafael and her son were playing with the puppy. When the girl was out of earshot, the hunchback said, *"Yo soy una moza soltera."*

I was no more at ease than the old woman who said yes, yes, to everything, and I had already nodded and smiled before I translated that unfamiliar phrase to myself. *I am a single maiden,* she had said. An unmarried girl? I put it out of my mind, and heard the tail end of her promise that her brother would soon be there. "I was coming in from the field and Carlito went out to tell them to come because there were visitors."

"You should not have done that," I said; "I am putting you to too much trouble."

"No, no," all of them said, not all at once, but in a kind of counterpoint.

73

"What marvelous faces!" my wife said. "You must take their photograph."

But I was ashamed to, and I said, "And this Dolores Andeiro and her son, did they live here?"

"Oh no, in Fuenfría," said the hunchback. "She lived in Fuenfría."

They saw in my reaction that something had again gone wrong, but they did not understand why. They didn't know that the address to which my mother used to write was not for Fuenfría, but for Miamán.

"She lived here until she got married," the hunchback said. "And then she moved to Fuenfría."

"Before my grandmother married, her name was Dolores Andeiro," I said, and the old woman nodded. "Her husband was named Yglesias." And I looked around at the unresponding faces. "And she also had a daughter."

"She came later," the old woman said, and chuckled.

"Yes, she was younger than the son," I said. "And she died soon after he did. Of tuberculosis."

"A weak chest," said the old woman. "She had a weak chest, Remedio."

But I didn't know whether that was my aunt's name; I could not at that moment remember if my mother had ever mentioned it. And I was still not sure that the things these lovely people told me were not bits of information which I had supplied them. Lovely people they were, however, and I had the feeling I was acting badly, that in not accepting them at their word, in not embracing them as cousins, as they seemed at each turn of the conversation ready to do with me were not I and my wife and son

74

such rich, forbidding people, I was acting more than badly by my standards; I was acting very American.

I unzipped the camera. "Here, I want to take your picture," I said, to make up for my bad faith.

Again the protestations: it was too fine a gift to accept, their very tones said. And the women were ashamed of their dresses. Only the old couple were complacent and made themselves ready; they probably had no new clothes: it is not a practical expenditure, not when you are waiting to die. I called Carlito, the boy with the patched pants; he was kneeling in front of a shed, showing Rafael what was inside, but he came when Rafael ran to me. "Daddy," Rafael said in an intense whisper, "they've got little pigs and rabbits in there!"

When I looked at the group through the viewer, I saw a row of serious people holding their breath; immobile, they had folded their hands in their laps, their eyes unblinking, except for Carlito, who stretched one hand toward a patched knee and whose eyes moved shyly from me to Rafael to my wife: Carlito, the son of an unmarried maiden. I saw him diminished but intensified through the camera's viewer, caught yet moving in his world, the way the poet Rosalía de Castro, herself a bastard child, pictured her own children playing in the garden, in one of her last anguished poems:

> In their jail of thorns and roses
> my poor children sing and play . . .
>
> In their jail they sleep and dream:
> how beautiful the cruel world they have not seen,

how broad the earth, how deep the seas,
how grand is space, how close their yard.

My wife suggested to the little hunchback that she keep
on the wide-brimmed straw hat, but she wouldn't; it was
just a work hat, to keep the sun out of her eyes in the
fields, not the elegant adornment my wife thought. When
I stood up, they immediately did too, and beyond them,
around one corner of the loaded wagon, approached a
man whose manner told me he was the master of the
house. And his deep, dark eyes, high cheekbones, dark
brown hair told me he was the hunchback's brother, the
robust middle-aged son of the attenuated old man still sitting in the upright chair under the apple tree. He extended
his hand and said, "Carlos Andeiro, to serve you," and
smiled and for a flickering moment became like his shy
adolescent nephew. His hand was massive, and though he
made no effort, his grip was numbing.

I told him my story and everyone stood by in a circle
and listened to it again. He *was* the master of the house,
and they waited for him to speak. "Then you come from
Cuba?" he said.

I said no, and explained about Florida, that it is close to
Cuba but in the United States, another nation. It seemed
to mean nothing to him; we were all disappointed.

Then he said, "You do not know Cousin Esperanza in
Havana?"

"Esperanza!" I exclaimed: she was the daughter of the
uncle of my father's with whom we had stayed in Havana
when I was a boy.

"Hope?" said my wife, translating the name, thinking it was a common noun.

"My cousin in Havana!" I said, and everyone leaned toward me to understand the English I had just spoken. I said to Carlos Andeiro, "You know Esperanza?"

"Cousin Esperanza, of course," he said. "She was here. She came to visit us and stayed here." He started to walk back to the house. "Wait, I shall bring you a photograph of her."

I sat down and saw him go into the dark house. I had forgotten about Esperanza; I had not thought of mentioning her, for we had lost touch with her many years ago, and her name was the first fact that these people had supplied me without a clue from me. Was it a coincidence? We all waited but we were all sure. Ana crossed herself. The little hunchback suddenly laughed. With her right forefinger she traced the line of her thick eyebrows, unbroken at the bridge of her nose. "Like my brother," she said, nodding toward the house. "And like you," she said, pointing to me. "It is the mark of the Andeiros!"

"Yes, yes!" I said, wanting to believe but remembering that I inherited my mother's eyes.

And she convinced my wife, who said, "It's true!"

But I waited for Carlos Andeiro; he came straight to me with an old photograph set in a gray cardboard frame. It was not the snapshot I expected, but a studio photograph, perfectly kept although at least half a century old. Not of Esperanza but of a young man standing by a chair, not yet bearded enough for there to be shadows on his face, wearing a high white collar, a suit with a four-button jacket, and holding a straw hat in his left hand between thumb and forefinger, as if he were going to fling it at me like a boomerang. Carlos Andeiro watched me stare at it and then placed the photograph in my lap and said quite simply, as if advancing an argument which had nothing to do with me, "This is the son of Aunt Dolores."

I had never seen that photograph but I knew the man: he was my father. I leaned over the photograph a moment, controlling an indescribable longing to kiss it, and heard my wife call out, "It's your father, it's exactly like him!" When I looked up, all their faces looked back at me eagerly. "Cousins!" I yelled it to keep from crying, and went from one to the other kissing them, leaning low to kiss the little hunchback. "I am Asuncion, Asuncion," she said, and I turned to the woman who had first taken us into the house and said, "And you are—" "Ana," she said, and the tears welled over and ran down her cheeks. Carlos Andeiro put each of his enormous hands on my shoulders and said, "Cousin!"

"You will eat with us," Ana said. "I shall go inside now and fix some eggs."

"Wait," I said. "You must each tell me your names." I took out a small notebook and pen, and they stood still and watched me as if I were taking their photograph. "I am too excited," I explained, and they all laughed, "and if I do not write down your names I shall forget or mix them up."

The men told me their names first and then the women, and when I got to Asuncion, the unmarried maiden, I was sorry, but she recited her name without any self-consciousness about lacking a married surname. I hurried over it and turned to Ana and said, "You are Ana Andeiro, right?" And she shook her head. "I am Ana Feijoo." "But you are—" I said, turning to Carlos Andeiro. He nodded and said, "My wife." And thus they explained the first mystery: why my grandmother always kept her maiden name. Without being feminists, the women in Galicia, or at least Miamán, did not adopt their husbands' names. And thus that niche in the churchyard wall which my wife discovered must have been my grandmother's.

The wonder of it made me silent, and when I came out of my reverie, I realized that they had been silent too, looking at the piece of paper on which I had written their names as at the working of magic. Writing them down with my miraculous literacy had put a distance between us.

"It is very little to offer you," said Ana Feijoo politely, using the formal *usted,* not the familiar *tu,* "but you will eat some eggs with us?"

I protested, using *tu* in such a way that I was saying we are cousins and you must not address me formally, and trying at the same time to do the right thing by refusing, for I knew that in Spain hospitality is demeaned if too easily accepted. I had seen Ana Feijoo's kitchen and knew the trouble it would be for her to cook for us. And my wife, catching the gist of what she proposed, said, "Oh no, no."

"You cannot stay?" Carlos Andeiro asked, still calling me *usted,* as deferential as if he had not shown me the photograph of the son of Aunt Dolores or grabbed my shoulders and called me cousin. It broke my heart: it was not a matter of suppressing a laugh, as when the bank clerks in Asturias called me Don Jose, but of not losing my newfound cousins, and not letting them be awed by me. Whatever I looked like, I was not that *usted* they addressed so respectfully.

I had to say that we would like very much to stay, and Ana Feijoo went off happy. I explained that we had taken a taxi and that it was waiting on the highway. They were impressed—it was hard to say anything that did not make them feel how extraordinary we were—but after a while, Asuncion asked, "Have you paid the driver?"

"No," I said, "but we have already come to an agreement about how much it will be."

"But you have not paid him the money?"

"No."

"Then he will wait," she said, and laughed shrilly. And then looked at me as if wondering whether she could dare ask how much it was going to cost me.

I laughed, remembering my plans for lunch in Miamán. The yard was full of sunlight and the smell of hay and drying earth, and my cousins looked at me and smiled. Here we are! And then the questions began: "Did my grandmother live here? And my father?"

Carlos Andeiro said she was born here and lived in this house until she married. "This is the principal house of the Andeiros," he said proudly, and we all turned to look at the long, cavelike house into which Ana Feijoo had disappeared to prepare a few eggs.

"Then this house goes back . . ."

"Oh many, many years," Carlos said and stopped, and I had the sense that he did not know, not the way we know, about the passage of time. "The grandparents, her grandparents, or maybe the parents of her grandparents were the first to move into this house. It belonged to the Valles and it is still known as the house of the Valles." He pointed to it with an outstretched arm. "It is an old house," he said happily.

"And my father?"

"When your grandmother married, she moved to Fuenfría and that is where your father was born."

"And when he came back?" I asked. Later, when I was back in Santiago, I remembered that Carlos hesitated and looked aside, waiting, I thought, until I made my question clear. "Is that where he lived before he went to the hospital?"

Asuncion broke in. "Aunt Dolores moved from Fuenfría later. She had bought some lands in Nodar," she said, looked quickly at her brother Carlos, and then hurried as if to cover her tracks, "because she had to, that is why, and that is where she died, in Nodar."

I only had time to think that the old woman did not, after all, live in Miamán most of her life, when I saw a man make the same turn into the yard as we had earlier. He was very thin, unshaven, the skin over the high cheekbones so fleshless that the eyes were set in deep hollows, and he smiled in anticipation and hurried across the yard toward me. He was frighteningly skeletal and in a moment he would be upon me. His face, as he put one arm around me, was a grinning skull. "Ramon, man, how are you!" he said.

The others called out to him, "No, no, it is the grandson of Aunt Dolores!"

"No!" the man said, and pulled back a little to get a good look at me, but kept his arm on my shoulder and a hand in mine. "I thought you were Esperanza's brother."

His voice was kindly and I knew my panic was caused by my unexpected recognition of that emaciated face: it was the face of my father on the pillow of the hospital bed in Havana, obliterated by the years, remembered by me only by the feel of his scratchy beard. I embraced him then and he was very pleased.

"Your mother made many efforts to get your father back," he said. "She went to Cuba when he was there."

"I was there with her," I said.

"That is right, I remember," he said. "I went to Cuba too."

I asked him if he had been there then, and he said no. "I went to Cuba after your father came back here. He was suffering from paralysis and when I came back in 1929, he was already dead."

I did not tell him that my father did not die until 1931, that in 1929 he was already in the hospital in Santiago. "And you are . . . ?" I asked.

"Jose Sabell, carnal cousin of your father."

"Another cousin!" I exclaimed, and they rushed to tell me that I had many more. My grandmother was one of six children and Miamán was full of my relatives.

"I want to meet them all," I said, and told them I had

come expecting to find none. "What about the Yglesi-
ases?" I asked, for no one had said anything about them.
"Are there any relatives of my grandfather's in Miamán?"

They looked at one another. "No, from that family they
have all moved away or died," Carlos finally said. "And
your mother? How is your mother? And you had a
sister?"

I told them, and wondered what they visualized.

Asuncion, the little hunchback, was the first to exclaim,
"Aunt Dolores used to worry about her and about her
grandchildren in America! Oh my grandchildren, my poor
grandchildren, she used to say."

Carlos said, "Aunt Dolores used to say what a good
woman her daughter-in-law was, because she wrote her
such affectionate letters."

"Oh yes," said Asuncion, "all those letters, and Aunt
Dolores had her grandchildren on her mind all the time,
especially when she got old."

At first I only caught one fact: my grandmother had
talked about us. Did she talk about us? I asked in order to
hear it again. "Oh yes, oh yes . . ." said the old woman
whose memory had turned out to be not so good. I looked
about at the others, and they nodded in reply. Behind
them I saw Rafael running with a long smooth branch in
both hands, tilting at the haystack; Carlito watched him
with an indulgent smile, like a grownup for whom such
pleasures are no longer possible.

The old woman called out something in such excited
Galician that I could not make it out. "What did she say?"
I asked, and Asuncion reprimanded her mother, remind-

ing her that she should speak in Castilian. "Please forgive her," she said to me. And Carlos explained, "Your father too, she said. He used to talk about his children, especially when he came back the second time."

"It was an effort for him to speak," Jose Sabell said, and brought a hand to his throat, as if that had been a characteristic gesture of my father's.

I sat down on the fallen tree trunk. All of them spoke at once, loud, shrilly, the Galician canceling out the Castilian. I came out of it, and asked, "What? What did you say?" They didn't want me to be sitting on the tree trunk: I must take one of the good chairs. I did what they said, and tried to start from the beginning. "Tell me," I said, "everything about my grandmother."

Carlos Andeiro thought it over. "She was a fine woman. Everyone liked her."

The old woman, Carlos Andeiro's mother, called out something again. "What?" I asked.

Carlos interpreted: "She was a lively woman, very gay and hardworking." And the old woman looked at me with a jolly expression and nodded.

"Yes?" I said.

"And when she married she went to live at Fuenfría . . ."

To encourage Carlos, I said, "And had a son and a daughter named . . ." I couldn't remember her name.

"Remedio Andeiro," said Carlos.

"Remedio Yglesias," I corrected.

Carlos shook his head. "Remedio was born when Aunt Dolores was a widow. When Aunt Dolores was an unmarried maiden again . . ." He smiled and looked at me as if saying, We men know about these things: we are to blame.

"Yes," I said, not knowing how else to respond. "Remedio died two years after my father and that was the last time we heard from my grandmother."

Carlos said nothing and his face said nothing.

I remembered what I wanted to ask him when I sat down on the tree trunk. "Why didn't my grandmother write to us again? My mother wrote to her several times and never got an answer."

Carlos looked aside, and the others, like him, did not seem to know what to say. I sighed involuntarily, and said, "All these years we thought she was all alone before she died." And I was immediately sorry, for it might sound like a criticism of them.

"Well, I suppose you know that Aunt Dolores did not know how to write," Carlos said, "and it was her brother-in-law, my uncle, who wrote the letters for her and read the replies. And when he died, I suppose there was no one. The women cannot read or write, you know that?"

Asuncion had her way of contradicting him. "Aunt Dolores had to work very hard. She had Claudio and Gustavo to bring up too."

I asked who Claudio and Gustavo were, and they were astonished. "Your carnal cousins," said Carlos.

"Remedio's?" I said.

"You do not know Claudio Balan and Gustavo Andeiro?" he said to me, and saw that I did not, and looked at me again and saw also that I did not know one was illegitimate. So he added, "When her husband died, Remedio had Gustavo years later. Like Aunt Dolores." And he put his head to one side and smiled again, painfully this time, as if he now suspected that where I came from illegitimacy was not a good thing.

My wife touched my elbow. "I have two first cousins!" I said to her in English, and left the rest for later.

"But you are staying in Santiago," said Carlos, "and you do not know El Gran Derby?"

"El Gran Derby?" I said, and shook my head.

"El Gran Derby belongs to Gustavo Andeiro," he said. "Everyone knows it. You just ask anyone where El Gran Derby is and go see your cousin Gustavo. When we go to Santiago we always stay there. So should you. You should not be spending money at a pension—" He stopped and I could see him remembering that we were rich, so he added, "Or a hotel."

I explained that we had only been in Santiago one day and did not yet know the city, so Carlos told me that El Gran Derby was a bar and restaurant with furnished rooms upstairs. His sister Asuncion laughed at him. "They are probably staying at El Hostal!" she said, meaning the Renaissance palace which the tourism ministry had turned into a luxury hotel. I shook my head, and she was puzzled; later, she asked with curiosity how it could be that none of us wore wrist watches: didn't we own any?

There was so much to absorb—I needed time just to think about my grandmother and aunt both having illegitimate children—and each face in the yard was a distraction. "And the other one?" I said, trying to get at the facts, like a good American. "Where is my other cousin?"

"Claudio Balan?"

I nodded.

"Claudio lives in Nodar. He has a tavern and much land—" Carlos stopped short, then explained, "You have to have much land here to grow enough. But it is all spread about, some in the mountains, some in the valley —the Redistribution will change all that and maybe we shall get tractors . . ." He did not think I was interested, so he added, "Claudio is a good man."

"Yes, yes," the others said. "A wonderful man."

"They work very hard, he and his wife," Carlos said.

"And my grandmother had two boys to bring up after my father and his sister died?" I looked to Carlos for an answer.

"She was a live one, Aunt Dolores," said the old woman, "and she worked very hard."

"Of course, Claudio was already a young man—" Carlos said.

Asuncion, the little hunchback, would not let him put a good face on things. "But when the army took him she had to work all the land alone. Gustavo Andeiro was just a little boy then, good only to take care of the cows. Aunt Dolores had a hard life."

"That is true," said Jose Sabell, and Carlos did not deny it. He looked pensive and nodded and gazed away. He saw my wife walking to the orreo, the little slatted cabin on stilts where corn is stored, and it pleased him that it interested her. He turned toward her and so did Jose Sabell and the others, amused and flattered that the fine lady might want to see the corn bin. "Show it to her!" Asuncion urged.

"Would Cousin Elena like to see the orreo?" Carlos asked, looking at me.

"Oh yes!" my wife said.

They laughed and told one another that Cousin Elena actually wanted to climb the wooden stairs up to the corn bin and look inside. Imagine! They watched Carlos lead us up the steps to the narrow platform in front of the door to the cabin, and Asuncion called Carlito to take Rafael too. The boys and my wife walked into the bin, but while we were still out on the platform, I asked Carlos why my cousin Claudio had not been excused from military training to help the old woman.

"Oh, it was not military service like the boys do now; it was the Movement," said Carlos. The narrow platform forced us to stand close together, and Carlos had to pull back his head and shoulders to look at me. "Did you hear of our Movement?" he said with a quizzical look exaggerated in close-up. In Spain, the Movement was once synonymous with the Falange, but now that the fascist nature of the regime is being muted, it is used to refer amorphously to all the forces which fought the Republic and to the vague ideals which guide the Franco regime. "You know that we had a war here?" Carlos said.

I told him that I had heard of it, and tried to get away and not hear what he might say next. As I walked into the bin, Carlos told me that he too had been in the Movement.

The dry, aerated cabin was a beguiling bower, its clean

air sweetened by the corn; in its ambience there was no place for what Carlos had just said. Rafael was excited by it, and my wife looked at me with childish happiness. I knew what she was thinking: it was a perfect retreat, the kind we searched for in our adolescence, away from the family, a place to read on long afternoons. The ears of corn were dry and light and had achieved a high waxy fin‑ ish, and when my wife picked up one and said she wanted to take it to my mother, I laughed. "She would like to have it," she said, insisting on sentiment, and Carlos was so proud that he picked out bright-colored ones for her, turning them over carefully to make certain they were perfect.

I went out to the platform alone to think about Claudio Balan and Carlos Andeiro having fought for the fascists. On this edge of the yard, the platform served as a balcony on the valley; the day was clear and I could look down to the thin highway two miles away and up to the mountains on the other side. Beyond the pine forest through which we had walked there were reddish tiled roofs among the trees. My thoughts would not stick; I could not make them real. So I said to Carlos when he came out, "Where did you fight during the war?"

"Oh, I was lucky," he said. "We were always in the mountains, scattered about and standing guard, and there was practically no fighting."

"Where?" I asked.

"One place to another," he said. He thought hard for a moment. "The first winter I spent in the mountains around Huesca," he said. "It was very cold."

"Ah!" I exclaimed, remembering George Orwell's winter there, and Carlos looked surprised. I turned away from him, and the green valley, the pine and eucalyptus forest, all turned into a bare, bony landscape, that winter scene of damp and desolation and high ideals which Orwell shared with his teenage, hungry, ill-equipped Anarchist comrades.

When I turned around, Carlos stood at the bottom of the wooden ladder helping my wife and the boys down. Except for the old man who remained placidly in his chair, no doubt stunned by the events of the day, the others behind Carlos called out admonitions, worrying about every step Cousin Elena took down the ladder. I stood alone at the top of the steps when a tall, thin peasant woman hurried into the yard, her hands clasped before her, and called in a thin shriek, "It is he, it is he!" Then pointed at me: "The son of Aunt Dolores himself!" I came down self-consciously, wondering who had informed her, for I had always been told that it was my sister and not I who resembled my father. She grabbed me and kissed me, saying in the same shrill voice, as if I were a block away, "It is his ghost come back from the grave!"

Close up I saw she had no teeth, just a solitary incisor which had snagged her lower lip and cut it. The others were embarrassed, and Jose Sabell, who was her brother, said impatiently, "Calm down and talk Castilian. Look, you have cut your lip." She paid no attention but stared into my face, her hands still clasped, as if I were a statue on an altar. Asuncion tugged at her elbow. "Wipe your mouth, woman," she said. "You are bleeding."

Ana Feijoo, Carlos' wife, came out of the house and saved them all from the problem of Jose Sabell's sister. The food was ready now, she announced, and then looked apologetically at us and said, "Just a little bite to eat, some eggs, that is all. Another time we shall treat you better." And she looked at my wife, her head to one side asking to be forgiven. The men picked up the chairs in the yard, and the group of us walked in a body to the house.

This time the inside seemed less strange. They made us sit at the table and Carlos and the old man joined us, but the others sat on the bench along the wall and watched us. Carlito sat at the end of the bench next to the open fire and his big eyes went from one to the other at the table and I knew what he was thinking: I remembered how, during the depression, I envied each member of my family and each person on the block as each left for New York to look for a job; I felt certain that I would never get out of Tampa, that the big important world would always be out of my reach.

I remonstrated with them: weren't they all going to eat with us? They assured me that they would be eating too, but that we would all be more comfortable this way. No, no, my wife said, we must not get special treatment. There were several more exchanges of that kind, but, of course, the arrangements remained as they had planned them. The protestations served, as they always have since Spaniards invited the first guest into their home, to clear the air, to make those getting second best feel that they had freely chosen it and to allow the guest to show that he is unworthy of the special attention.

Ana Feijoo served us a potato omelette, broiled sausages, and glasses of thick, tart Galician wine; she brought a large round loaf of bread to the table, and Carlos cut enormous slices from it, holding it against his chest and cutting toward it. They were proud of what they were serving us, and they should have been: the omelette was delicious and the sausages the best I had ever eaten. "We make them ourselves," Carlos said, and to hear us say it again, he asked, "Do you find them good?"

While we ate, Carlos told us that living conditions were now better. They had electricity and a radio, and everyone in Miamán had agreed to the Redistribution, so that perhaps soon they would have a road coming from the top of the mountain down through Miamán all the way to the highway. Then the government might give them loans, so that they could buy a tractor; as it was, with each farmer's lands scattered in different places, with no roads to drive from one plot to the other, and without credit toward the purchase price, tractors were out of the question. Ah yes, life was much better now.

"This is delicious bread," I said.

And that was too much for Asuncion, the little hunchback, who had been frowning throughout Carlos' talk. "That is wheat bread!" she said, as if proving a point. "Let me show you what we eat most of the time, and all of the time in winter when the wheat runs out!" She dashed toward the front corner of the room; I turned away from the table to look back at her and was thus able to see the grimace she made for Ana Feijoo's benefit: I'll show them, her face said, since they are so rich, just what poverty is.

She brought out a hard half loaf whose dough was the gray color of cornbread, and she forced it into my hand. "It is made of *maíz,* such as we feed the pigs!" Carlos looked down at his plate, and beyond his bowed head I saw the shamed look on Ana Feijoo's face. Asuncion had wiped out the lovely lunch she had prepared.

The bread weighed like a stone in my hand. "In New York where we live," I said, "there are some bakeries which make bread with a corn dough as a specialty. It costs more than the other breads made with wheat."

The information made Carlos look up but it did not entirely dispel the effect of Asuncion's outburst. She sat on a bench next to Carlito, and Ana Feijoo handed everyone, except us, their lunch: a plate overflowing with rice and beans. In the dim room, I could not immediately make out what it was, and Ana Feijoo insisted on giving me some when I asked. I liked it and so, gradually, we were all happy again.

When I asked the time, they told me it was three o'clock, and we jumped up and said we had to leave. I promised I would come back; we had made arrangements to leave for La Coruña in two days, but we were coming back to Santiago for a longer stay. "When would it be best to come back to Miamán?" I asked, and Carlos assured me that any day we would be welcome. We were so courteous on either side—he not wanting to insist or set any limits, we not wanting to impose or put them to expense by giving them advance warning—that the arrangements remained vague.

The old man apologized for not going with us down to

the highway—he had to lie down to catch his breath—but Carlos insisted on coming with us: he knew a shortcut. Before we left the house, he went to a door in the passageway along the wall behind me and with a happy smile said, "These are our oxen!" He pulled open the door and there, in a long low barn, were two oxen resting, like members of the family in a bedroom of their own. He stepped in, stroked one on its flanks, and the oxen got up —my wife was right—ready to serve us: so said their clear brown eyes.

"They are very good animals, aren't they?" my wife said, and I translated.

Behind us Ana Feijoo sighed, and Carlos grasped the horn of the nearest ox and said, "Oh, they are very good, they work very hard for us," and laughed when we said they were also beautiful to look at.

We said goodbye to everyone in the doorway, and followed Carlos across the yard to the shortcut to the highway. Ana Feijoo first waved at us, then quickly caught up with us as we began to climb down to the fields. She touched my wife's arm so that she too would listen. "If we have done anything wrong, if we have offended you in any way," she said, "please forgive us. We are ignorant and do not know how to act." Then she watched us go with tears in her eyes. My wife looked up once after we had navigated the slope, and Ana Feijoo waved and crossed herself.

In the middle of the field of corn seedlings, Carlos pointed up to the hills I had looked at from the platform

of the orreo, and said that up there was where Claudio
Balan lived. "That large house, the tallest one you see, is
his," he said.

"I thought you said he lives in Nodar," I said. "In another aldea."

"Nodar is Miamán," he said, and looked at me closely,
as when he had explained about the Movement. "Did I
not tell you that? That we could walk there?—it is a part
of Miamán we all call Nodar." He explained this while we
stood in the field, and I could see that he now understood
why I had not asked to be taken there, why I had acted so
coldly about Claudio Balan, for he was my carnal cousin
and carnal cousins are the same as brothers.

"And Fuenfría?" I said.

"Is just below Nodar," he said. "You cannot see it because of the trees."

"Then my father's house . . ."

"Is there," he said. "It is still there."

We stopped a moment longer, all in a row looking up at
the trees. "Then I surely must come back," I said.

Carlos clapped me on the back. "That you must do, man,"
he said. "I shall go tonight and tell Claudio that you want
to meet all your relatives."

Once we left the tilled fields, we walked in the woods.
At one point, we came to a brook which led to a clearing;
on level ground, still shaded by the trees nearby, was a
wooden, one-room building which looked like a New England meetinghouse, except that it was unpainted. Carlos
stopped a moment and looked around. "This is where we

hold our *romerías*," he said, and smiled a man's smile which was just for me. "If only you could stay until next month!"

"They are very gay, aren't they?" I said.

He lifted his eyebrows, then nodded emphatically. "They start in the morning and go on until the next day. We eat and drink and sing and dance and everyone goes to sleep wherever they drop."

The clearing was peaceful and quiet now. I remembered the writer in Madrid who had said, "In Galicia you must go to the romerias during the summer—they are pagan for all that they are supposed to celebrate the patron saint of the village." I took a good look at the clearing and tried to see the girls of Miamán in red and white dresses with black aprons (*Light feet/ Erect body,* said Rosalía about them) and to listen to the bagpipes playing. I was sure it was here that my grandmother and my aunt and the little hunchback Asuncion had, as the Latins in Tampa say, forgot themselves.

4

In the taxi, our visit began to seem real: our shoes were caked with red mud, the bright ears of corn stuck out of my wife's bag, and Rafael informed us that Carlito had offered him the furry puppy to take back to America. Carlos had told the driver to take us directly to El Gran Derby, but on the way to Santiago I changed those instructions. I asked the driver to show us El Gran Derby and then drive us on to our hotel where we planned to bathe and rest before we went out to meet the younger of my carnal cousins. The little Plaza San Lazaro where El Gran Derby was situated could not be entered by car, for the granite paving was being replaced and workmen sat on the ground, chisel in hand, shaping the granite blocks much as it had been done centuries ago when they were first laid. From the taxi we saw the little black and white sign of El Gran Derby over the doorway of one of the little buildings; it was obviously a place where workmen could enter for their penny glass of white wine without any self-consciousness.

In the hotel, I took out my father's photograph, and after looking at it again, I told my wife that Carlos Andeiro, the kind man who had given it to me and who had picked out the ears of corn for her, had fought for the fascists. And so had Claudio Balan, the carnal cousin whom we had yet to meet in Miamán. It was not until I was telling her this that I realized my grandmother had lived for many years after her last letter arrived in Tampa. There were other things, I saw now, that the Andeiros had left unsaid: that none of them had seen my father in the hospital nor been to his funeral, nor knew where he was buried. The poor are forced to forget their own: what an enormous effort it must have taken in those days to go from Miamán to Santiago! Yet they had kept his photograph . . .

Drums and bagpipes sounded from below, and from our narrow balcony over the medieval street we watched an unexpected parade. A band of drums and bagpipes preceded a long contingent of university cadets in brilliant uniforms. Four abreast, they filled the old street from one end to the other, and marched smartly under us on the way to the cathedral.

"Don't think about what they signify," my wife said. "Just enjoy it."

We did not know that Claudio Balan's son was one of those cadets nor that Claudio himself had come in from

Miamán to see him parade. When we saw them make the
turn at the end of the street and disappear, we went down
to walk to El Gran Derby. It was five thirty and the workmen were still chipping at upright granite blocks outside;
one of them sat with a red-haired woman just inside the
doorway of El Gran Derby, at a tiny table across from a
tiny bar. The light from the doorway was quickly blotted
by the implacable darkness of the long room beyond, for
there were no windows and the room received no other
natural light. Just beyond the bar where the light died,
rows of long, oilcloth-covered tables and benches on either side of them crouched like dim bulks; a center aisle
led to a shallow kitchen, set off by low partitions, but you
could see none of this without squinting.

A short thin man, who had been standing at the bar
talking to the dust-covered workman and the woman at
the table, walked behind the bar when we entered. He
looked pale, unlike the peasants in Miamán, and his face
was permanently creased with worry. I took ten years off
his appearance, and figured he was in his late thirties. An
inquiring look flickered on his face, and he said, "Good
day," hesitantly, as if he were not sure that the foreigners
would understand. His relief at my ordering in Spanish
—one Pepsi-Cola and two espressos—was immediately
tempered by his having to say they did not have coffee. It
was a poor bar, either because they could not afford a
coffee machine or because their customers could not
afford coffee, which is three times more expensive than
white wine. So I ordered three Pepsis; they were *al*

tiempo, room temperature, which is how Spaniards often drink it, but at El Gran Derby there was no choice because there was no refrigerator or ice at the bar.

I paid him as soon as he served us, something which is not done and which he must have attributed to our being foreigners. I put the change away and paused a moment and looked around. The workman and the red-haired woman returned my look with interest; she wore a fringed black wool shawl crossed over her buxom chest, the ends tucked into her skirt. She smoothed it carefully, moved her head a little to make sure her dangling earrings were still on, and continued studying us. "Are you named Gustavo Andeiro?" I said to the man behind the bar, and the lines on his face became exclamation points.

"Yes!" he said.

"Well," I said, "I am your cousin from America."

I extended a hand over the bar to shake his, and he took it and looked at me furtively to see if he had a drunk customer on his hands. "You do not believe me," I said, "but we are cousins, carnal cousins at that."

"If you say so," he said and smiled, and looked over at the couple at the table and raised his shoulders and grinned.

"Remedio, your mother, was my father's sister," I said, and he began to listen very carefully, "and my father, who was your uncle, married in America and had two children."

I waited while he stared and searched his memory. "Remedio was my mother's name," he said.

I laughed. "You do not believe me, but I have just come

from Miamán and Carlos Andeiro told me I would find you here."

"You were in Miamán!" he said, as if that were more astonishing than our relationship.

"That is how I knew how to find you. I have to confess that until today I did not know that I had cousins in Spain." He did not take his eyes off me, but he said nothing. "Did you know that your uncle had children in America?"

He looked down and considered the question, as if his opinion had been asked on a serious subject about which he had not often thought. "I must say to you that I did not know." And then we were both silent.

"Oh Holy Mary!" exclaimed the red-haired woman and drew the shawl more tightly across her bosom. "I knew that today was the day to come in from the aldea. I knew that something good would happen!"

Gustavo Andeiro was still thinking over this extraordinary thing that had happened, and it seemed to present itself to him as a problem, as if he had run out of wine to serve his customers. He did not shake my hand again, nor did he come out from behind the bar and embrace me. I introduced my wife and son, and he nodded to them; his gaze lingered longer over Rafael to make up for the briefness of his shy look at my wife.

"I tell you it gives me hope," the red-haired woman said, and when the workman chuckled and winked at me, she added, "Pay no attention to him, he is my husband and has no sympathy. One day, I swear, my old man will walk into the aldea and say, Here I am. He left for America when I was two and we have never heard from him again, the old bastard. Excuse my being so frank."

We all laughed, except Gustavo Andeiro: she was just a tiresome customer to him.

"Listen, where in America does your father live?" the woman asked me.

I told her that I lived in the United States but that my father was dead and had died here in Santiago. I watched Gustavo as I said it, and saw that all this was news to him.

"That is where my father went!" she said, and told me his name, hoping I might know him. "How I would like to see him! My sister who was only a few months old when he left says it is of no consequence to her—she says she does not care whether she is the daughter of the village priest. Not me, I want to know what my old man is like, and I have not given up hope." She leaned across the table and slapped her husband on the shoulders. He smiled and showed his toothless but healthy gums.

Finally, Gustavo asked, "And what are you doing in Spain?"

I told him. I said that in Miamán they did not seem to know where my father died or where he was buried, and that I wanted to see those places.

"I have to tell you," he said, as if he were dealing with a salesman he had to turn down, "that I do not know anything about all that. I was too young, I do not remember hearing anything about it."

I looked into the interior of the restaurant; it depressed me and so did the reception my cousin had given us. "Our grandmother never spoke about her grandchildren in America?" I asked, with no apology for my directness.

Gustavo shrugged his shoulders. Then a slow smile came over his face, not impulsive enough, however, to make him part his lips. "It may be, it may be," he said, looking inward. "I have the feeling that I knew, but you know boys, they never listen to the adults."

An adolescent girl appeared in a doorway behind the red-haired woman, and Gustavo told her, with all the harshness of an order, to go back upstairs and tell Luz to come down. "She is putting the baby to sleep," said Gustavo to me, and his face softened. "We have a baby boy and a girl four years old." The young girl still stood in the doorway staring at us, and Gustavo said, "Go on up and tell her to come down."

The red-haired woman called after the girl: "Tell her a cousin from America is here."

The workman shook his head complacently and said to me, "This woman cannot mind her own business."

His wife laughed good-naturedly. "You are giving the gentleman the wrong impression. Luz and I are from the same aldea." She appealed to me: "You see him here drinking?—he should be outside working."

Her husband took off his wide-brimmed straw hat and stroked his bald head. "The day is about over, woman."

"Listen," she said to me, with an emphasis which showed she was going to ask a favor, "do you know the Casa Ford in New York City? The last time I heard about my father he was working there. He had a fine position fixing cars."

"Aie-yay-yay!" said the workman. "There she goes!" He finished up the little glass of white wine and got up to leave, pretending he was driven out by his wife's talk.

We all laughed at that, her laughter louder than the rest; even Gustavo laughed, only he looked down, a little embarrassed that I should be hearing all this, and suddenly I realized that Gustavo was not cold but shy. And when his wife Luz appeared in the midst of the laughter, looking like a city girl, I saw that he was drawn to warm-hearted women. Luz greeted us like the girl from the aldea that she used to be before they moved into Santiago: she took my hand in both of hers and exclaimed, "A cousin!" and kissed my wife and ran her hands through Rafael's hair and looked him up and down lovingly.

"Maria said there was a cousin from America downstairs and I did not believe her! And your wife, she too is Spanish . . . ? But she understands it? What a marvel! But what are they doing standing up—you did not make them sit down! But Padrino was here today and he did not tell us about you. . . . Then you have not met him— Padrino is Claudio, his older brother and your cousin and a wonderful man, and we call him Padrino because he is also my husband's godfather and benefactor and he is all that to me too. And Isabel, his wife, you did not meet her in Miamán? She is a saint and I love her and you shall love her too."

While she talked she got us seated and, without our noticing, got Gustavo to open three more bottles of Pepsi-Cola and place them in front of us. "Oh Soledad," she said to the red-haired woman who came from the same aldea as she, "is this not a lovely happening, that we should gain such beautiful cousins without our having done anything to deserve it?"

"Listen, Luz, this is a lucky day for me too," said Soledad, whose name means solitude and was most inappropriate. "Do you know your cousin lives in New York City and will find my father for me when he returns? That old bastard! God forgive me, but the truth is the truth."

Soledad's husband still stood in the doorway; it was all too interesting to leave, and he had to step in again to make way for two workmen who came in and watched us. Gustavo went behind the counter and, without asking, put two little glasses on the counter and gave the men a questioning look. They nodded and he filled them with white wine from a pitcher. We were all quiet for only a moment.

"What a pity that the baby is asleep and that Lucita is in the aldea with my mother this week," said Luz, and explained that Lucita was in Paramos, not Miamán, for like Ana Feijoo and Soledad, Luz came from Paramos.

Soledad said, "What a difference from the old days! Now that we have the Redistribution in Paramos and there are roads, we can come and go to Santiago with ease. Not that the Redistribution was not a headache for me! Let me tell you what happened, for it made me famous in Santiago. True, Luz?"

She did not really look at Luz or Gustavo for confirmation or she would have seen that they were casting about for an excuse to get us off somewhere alone. But Soledad was launched on her story and there was no stopping her.

"The case came to court here in Santiago and there are still law students at the university who remember it and when they see me in the street, on the occasions when I come to the city, they call out to me, Hello Soledad, have they given you your law degree yet?"

Having got our attention, she smoothed her shawl over her bosom, told her husband he did not have to stay for the story, and began at the beginning. When the Redistribution came to Paramos, the men of the aldea were required to put in time without pay to build roads, and like the others Soledad's husband was assigned to one group. But there was much jealousy because her husband, knowing the work better than the others, could not avoid arguments as to what should be done and who should do it.

"In any case," she laughed, "I walked out to where they were working one day and found that three of the men had set to beating my man!" She yelled at them but they paid no attention, so she picked up a branch of a tree and hit one man on the head; another she hit—she lifted one knee to show how she had done it—in "a bad place," and the man had to spend twelve days in a clinic. Her husband, I assumed, took care of the third man.

The persecution of her husband stopped, but the man who went to the clinic denounced her to the authorities and charges were brought against her. "Imagine, the announcement appeared in the newspaper saying I was accused of having injured a man—which written down in a newspaper is as good as true. It was then the law students became interested in the case.

"I do not have much commerce with priests but my

conscience began to suffer, for I had found out from one
of the students that if I told the truth I would be punished—imagine, what is the good of the truth if that is
what it gets you!—so I decided in desperation to go to
confession and get advice. I told the priest, in a word, that
I had committed the sin of which I was accused and that
it lay heavy on my heart, and he said to me, Well, my
daughter, what you have done is a mortal sin but you
have fulfilled your obligation to God by confessing it. You
do not have to condemn yourself in court, for what hap-
pens there is another matter! And he gave me his blessing
and hoped I would not be too long again in coming to
church. Such was my relief that I had to find a way to
thank God, and I gave a goodly sum to charity. I put it in
one of those boxes you always find at the church door
while the mood was upon me—for I had come prepared.

"So I went to court determined to defend myself. It was
filled, for the announcement again appeared in the papers
and the students and even the police of the court were on
my side. When my name was called—Soledad Sanchez
Miguez!—they all opened a way for me to walk through.
Are you willing, the judge asked me, to pay sixteen hundred pesetas damages for what you have done and five
hundred for medical costs? And I said, No, señor, for I am
innocent and insolvent. And that was the first time the
students laughed.

"I told the judge that there could have been no alterca-
tion for we all got along very well in the aldea, which was
true except for those envious persons who attacked my
husband, and he began to ask me other questions. He

wanted to know if someone had been in charge of the road work, and I knew what he was after—he was trying to see if my husband had refused to follow orders or had not cooperated. So I acted as if the question were not that and I told him that everyone was happy to work on the road because it was to benefit everyone. Yes, the judge said, but was there not one person above all the others? Oh señor, I said to him, everyone was right in there working away. So the judge began over again and said, I mean when a road or anything else is built, there is always someone who says to the others, put a brick here, another brick there and some sand someplace else, right? Was there not someone who made decisions like that for the men? he asked.

"I acted as if I now understood, and I said, Ah yes, señor, I see what it is you mean, but I do not know, for it is a well-known code of behavior—and one which I honor—that when men plan things, a woman's place is to stay out of it. Which is what I did, I said. This time the judge laughed along with the students and even the police of the court, and he gave up and said he hoped I would continue to act that way and he let me off. They tell me you could hear the laughter out in the street, and that is why when one of those students sees me now he calls out, Soledad, have you got your law degree yet!"

Soledad did not tell the story without a stop as I have put it down, for I occasionally had to translate it for my wife or to ask about some Galician word whose meaning I could not figure out. At first, Luz, Gustavo's wife, watched me with some apprehension, but she laughed along with us when she saw I enjoyed it, and even Gustavo smiled at the end.

"Oh Soledad," said Luz, "what will our cousin think when he hears stories like that? It will confirm all the bad things they tell about Gallegos."

Soledad threw up one hand and addressed us all, including the workmen crowding the bar. "But he is a Gallego himself!" she said, nodding at me. "Look at him, tall and broad-shouldered like any man from the aldea. A true Gallego!"

Yes, the men at the bar assured me, I was a true Gallego's son, and Luz came over to my wife and took her hand and then mine and she said that we must eat a little something. We began our protests, but she said we must not worry, it would only be a little bite. "You can go upstairs to the little dining room and Gustavo can sit and talk to you, now that he is free."

That last made us demur even more, for we realized they were working people and we were in the way. I proposed that we come back at nine in the evening and take them out to dinner. They both looked at us with an indulgent smile, and as Gustavo led us upstairs—narrow, medieval stairs, so that my shoulders touched the walls on either side—he explained their life to us. Their day ends at one in the morning, and he gets up early to buy food for the day and to open the bar and bring in ready-made coffee for the morning customers who have cafe au lait and a piece of bread; this last he sometimes leaves to Luz and the two young girls from her aldea who work for them. Many days they serve as many as 180 plates at lunchtime, for their regular student customers—three or four of whom live in the upstairs rooms—are joined in the middle of the day by workers who come into the city from the countryside; in the evening they serve as many as eighty. By the time the dishes are done and the place tidied for the next day, it is one in the morning, and the only break they get is from five to seven in the afternoon.

"We mainly get students," reported Gustavo very seriously; "they never have any money and they have time to investigate every restaurant in the city to find the cheapest with the best food. It is a hard life, but on Sundays for one reason and another there is not as much work."

"You are open on Sundays?" I said. "What day do you close?"

He stopped on the little landing of the second floor and thought it over. "We are going to close a few days this summer, maybe three or four whole days. We shall go to Villa Arosa and stay a whole weekend at a pension, so Luz will not have to cook. I am determined to do it, for we have worked five years without a stop."

Beyond the landing, past two closed doors, was a small dining room with two tables which together could seat about twenty people. "We serve here too," said Gustavo, and led us to the small one with chairs. In a moment, Luz and one of the girls brought platters of fried *merluza,* a delicious white fish, and salad and bread and Galician wine. No one paid attention to our protests, and I determined to eat until I was sick in order not to hurt their feelings. Gustavo paused before he poured the wine and asked if I liked Galician wine. I said yes enthusiastically, and he asked where I had first tasted it. I said Madrid, and he shook his head and said, "There already it is not quite as good as it should be, for the movement of transportation bruises it."

I told him I had also enjoyed it in Vigo and that it did taste better in Galicia. He shook his head again, though not as emphatically this time. "Vigo and La Coruña are right by the sea and that affects it too."

We drank the wine and took a bite of the fish; both were delicious, for Galicians simply do not know how to prepare fish badly. We were silent; it was due to sudden tiredness, Gustavo's and ours, and to my knowledge that there was nothing he could tell me about my father. He was not interested in the past and was too shy. He was interested in facts, I said to myself, and I looked at him and wondered how he had got into this business in the city; he looked pasty and thin in the clearer light of the dining room; there were deep lines in his forehead, and in his cheeks where dimples should have been; his arms were thin and knotted with prominent veins, and you knew that all his strength was in his nerves and determination.

Only yesterday my wife and I had laughed at a statue of Atlas which looks down from the top of an old building on Plaza Toral at the end of our street; he was a sad, wizened, old Atlas, and the world on his shoulders was an intolerable burden: it bent his knees, furrowed his brow and strained his sunken, thin belly, so that he seemed on the point of doubling up. But there was no suggestion in his worried eyes that he wanted help. Old Atlas stood his ground like a little boy in a street fight, holding back the tears, neither winning nor losing nor calling for his brothers. Such a marvelous image in art, such a sad fact in life.

I asked Gustavo about himself, remembering to say nothing which required acknowledgment of the fact that he still bore his grandmother's maiden name, that he could refer only to one parent out of two and one grandparent out of four. What interest could he have in the past? His life seemed to begin in 1953 when he went to Venezuela and stayed for four years. Padrino had given him the money to go, 15,000 pesetas, which if worth then what it is now ($250) was a lot of money; he always paused a little and let his voice go soft when he spoke Padrino's name. Padrino was Claudio Balan, his older brother who had the benefit of a legitimate surname, and who was my other carnal cousin, as Carlos Andeiro put it. Gustavo also mentioned a Madrina, a godmother, and for a while I thought she might be our grandmother, but I decided later she must be Claudio's wife, Isabel, whom Luz had called a saint.

The very day Gustavo's boat docked in Venezuela he got a job. "If I were to land in New York tomorrow," he said, "I would immediately have a job though I do not speak English, for they tell me that Americans refuse certain kinds of work and there is nothing I will not do." In Caracas, Gustavo saw a man sweeping the sidewalk outside a little bar-restaurant, and asked him if he did not need a man to do that and other work for him. That was his first job, but he kept his eyes open and soon learned it was in construction work that a man could earn real money. Gustavo had no intention of staying in Venezuela or spending the major part of his life away from Galicia, and he was determined to come back with money saved.

He did not have to become an apprentice in the building trades, for there was so much construction going on in Caracas that there was a shortage of trained hands; first, he studied the men who mixed the cement, and as soon as he thought he could do it, he went to another site and asked for that job. Finally, he was doing the most highly paid work in construction, standing on the skeletal girders and guiding into place the steel beams which the crane swung to him, and then welding them.

I said that was very dangerous work.

"I never looked down or up at the thing I was doing," he said, "and I never had an accident and it paid well."

There were weeks when he worked at this eighteen hours every day. He hugged a beam with one arm when there was a pause in the work, closed his eyes and dozed for a second. Before the first year was out, he had paid Padrino the money he had given him for the passage, and in four years he had put away almost five thousand dollars. On the way back to Spain, he stopped in Cuba, figuring that since it was closer to the United States there might be work in Havana which paid even more.

"But there was nothing doing there, with all those unions which keep a man from working," he said. "Anyway, they were not building anything, it was all gambling and tourism . . . and there was all that unrest."

"That must have been during Batista's last year," I said. "The revolutionaries were very active."

He shrugged his shoulders. "Whatever it was . . . I

did not like that country. I like it here where there is peace and you can go about your work."

Gustavo, you are a real Gallego, I said to myself, a man who cannot see beyond his nose or his little business. But I did not know what to do with that feeling and looked down at the worn oilcloth on the table as if I were thinking over his story: I reminded myself that Galicia had been a stronghold of Republicanism and the Franco army had been able to take the main cities mostly through trickery; the little plaza we loved in Vigo had been the scene of the Franco army marching in, during the first days of the uprising, with cries of *¡Viva la República!* when, in fact, they had come to destroy it.

Unaccountably, Gustavo broke the silence this time. "I remember as if in a dream the day my mother died," he said, and closed his small, tough, veined hand on the oilcloth. "I was working out in the fields and I could not have been more than five." He looked at me. "Or maybe four."

My wife could eat no more, and she was sitting back, having lost track of the conversation. But the change in Gustavo's tone made her look at me questioningly. "He lost his mother when he was four," I said, as if defending him.

"Her lungs were bad," he said, "but she did not stop working and went out in all kinds of weather. She had to work, I guess."

I told him she died two years after my father, and said I hoped to find out where he was buried. Also, where he had died.

He thought about it for a while and I waited for him.

"He must be buried in the holy ground in Miamán, just like my mother. She is buried there, I do not know exactly where," he said, and looked at me hoping I would understand. "Things were very bad in those days, we just kept alive. I do not know if there was even a marker on the ground for my mother. Now Padrino has a pantheon where our grandmother is buried."

I asked again if he had heard where my father was sent after the hospital would keep him no longer. First he shook his head, then he said there was a charity home called the Asylum of the New Road, a place you could see from the heights of the Horseshoe Park on the highway leading away from the city, once called the New Road. Then he said no more.

He must have read my thoughts, however, for he volunteered again that he was very young and that was why he had not known about my father. "True, when Grandmother died I was older, fifteen or perhaps sixteen," he said, "but even then you know how youngsters are, and if she talked about you and your sister and your mother I must not have listened."

"Then Grandmother lived until 1945 or 46!" I said.

But Gustavo did not know what that meant to me and said, "Yes, she lived to be well past eighty and she worked until the very end. There were times when Padrino was away in the army and she had only Madrina to help her."

As with the Andeiros, I told him I could not understand why she had stopped writing us so many years before that. "We could have helped," I said.

He did not know. "I did not know anything about you," he insisted.

He did not say that the old woman was illiterate, nor that her brother-in-law who wrote the letters died; he had no excuses like Carlos Andeiro, and in this small dark room, so unlike the lovely yard in Miamán, the bare truth was bleak.

Our conversation proceeded like an old train carrying unimportant cargo in a railroad yard, full of painful stops and starts. After a while, I asked, "How did you survive? Who took care of you?"

"Padrino and Madrina were like a father and mother to me," he explained, "and when Grandmother died I was already grown and I went to live with Padrino, who had married by that time."

"Isabel is not your godmother?"

He shook his head, but Isabel interested him very much. He told me how hard she and Claudio worked, and it seemed to me that he was measuring his and Luz's performance against theirs. "They have all that farmland and a tavern and they hire no one to work for them. They do it all themselves. And Isabel is a small, frail woman, and she has been very ill and yet she continues to work and work as in the old days." He screwed up his eyes and said, as if he had given it long thought, "When a woman is smart like Isabel, she can do more work than those who are only strong."

Then he told me a remarkable thing: Claudio's and Isabel's son Paco lived there with him and went to the university. He was their only child and had made the jump from peasant to *señorito*, a young gentleman attending the university like other *señoritos*. "Padrino came to see

him in the parade today," said Gustavo. "He has everything he needs, that boy. I do not know why Padrino and
Isabel work so hard."

"Miamán is a beautiful place," I said.

"The food is better but I would have to be hungry in-
deed," he said, "to go back there to work. There would
have to be absolutely nothing else I could do." Then he
permitted himself a smile to show me he was aware that I
now knew, after his story of his years in Venezuela, that
there was nothing he could not do. "I still have land in
Fuenfría. I have it farmed for me."

One of the girls from the aldea came up to clear our
table. We had tried hard but there was still much food
left, and we made many apologies. It was time to go, for it
was seven, when Gustavo would have to begin preparing
for the evening customers, and he did not hold us back. I
told him we would leave the next afternoon for La
Coruña and that we would be back in five days, for I
wanted to visit the municipal palace and find where my
father was buried. "Also, I want to visit Miamán again
and meet your brother Claudio."

On the little landing, he said to me, "If I could find a
male relative to leave here with Luz, someone who would
protect her only, for she knows how to run the business—
look how she has learned to cook for dozens of people
though she never did it in the aldea—I would like to visit
the United States."

"Good, good," I said. "It would make us so happy if you
visited us in New York and the family in Tampa."

But I was wrong: he wanted to spend time in the

United States to work. "I would not go as a tourist, never," he said, for he figured he could save more money there than he did in Venezuela.

Downstairs, the girls were getting the tables ready, and the air was heavy with the smell of cooking. There were men at the bar, and Luz stood behind the partition at the stove. We went to her and Gustavo left us to attend to the bar. Behind the partition, there were platters full of fish already dipped in flour, and in the cramped space Luz had only to reach behind her, without moving from her position in front of the tiny stove, to drop them into two frying pans smoking with oil. She giggled like a young girl when she saw us, as if we had caught her at play.

On Luz's face, wet with perspiration, was reflected the worry that if she stopped to wipe her face, if she talked, if she embraced us, the fish would burn. And she was also ashamed. So she laughed nervously again, and retrieved her floury hands which had instinctively started out to reach for ours and wiped them and called to one of the girls to watch the fish in the pans. We did not let her come out from behind the partition, and we promised her that in five or six days, when we returned from La Coruña, we would come to see her. She kept both hands on each of ours as we said goodbye, and she nodded at everything we said.

She would not turn her back and go to work until we turned our backs on her, so we started down the aisle to leave. The men already beginning to take their places at the tables looked at us with curious smiles, and one young man remained in the aisle and stopped us halfway. "I am Paco Balan," he said, and it took me a moment to realize this was my cousin's son. He held himself straight and spoke without any of the shrillness or Galician lapses of the people from the aldeas, but he had been working at the tables and his face and shirt were moist.

Paco had little of the self-assurance of the students of middle-class origin we saw in Madrid and Barcelona, nor the charm of the young men who marched under our balcony that afternoon. And he had learned to suppress the warmth of manner of his relatives in the aldea. He offered his services to us while we were in Santiago and then looked down as if we were sure to reject them; we made a date for the morning at our hotel to spend part of the day together, since we were not to take the bus until late afternoon. He stepped back slightly, brought his feet together and bowed from the waist, pleased with the honor.

As we walked toward the street, I took a look at Gustavo behind the bar; he was pouring wine from the little pitcher for the men crowding the doorway, his face again worriedly serious and creased, and although one of the men tried to get his attention to show him we were leaving, he did not look up. The sun was setting and the old stones of the little plaza were rosy and soft, and I wanted to look back into the dimly lit, bustling hole of a restaurant but did not do so because I felt sure they were all still watching us and would be embarrassed. I was sorry that I did not, for I might then have been able to put some distance between myself and my talk with Gustavo, a worri-some encounter at whose heart there was a nagging mystery which left me sad and unwelcome.

After we had walked the first block to our hotel, my wife said, to console me, "His wife Luz is lovely."

In a little while, I said, "There must've been *one* literate person in Miamán who could have written a letter for the old woman, don't you think?"

She shook her head, a form of advice. "Who can tell what happened . . . ?"

We planned to miss the paseo time and go up to our room and rest before dinner, and that is what my wife and Rafael did. I left them at the door to the hotel because I wanted to go to the Horseshoe Park and look for the Asylum of the New Road while there was still light. At the end of our street, one block past the square above which the harassed Atlas crouched, the streets of the old town emptied into the park. The *alameda,* a tree-lined walk in the form of a horseshoe which borders the park, is the goal of the strollers at paseo time; every Spanish town has its alameda, but Santiago's is especially enticing. At this eastern edge of the old town the land slopes steeply down into a farming valley, except for the park: it is like a stubborn peninsula of the old town, a promontory over the valley; at the horseshoe's bend you are highest over the valley, and as you turn the bend coming back you see, through arbors, and breaks in the trees, old Santiago itself with the cathedral at its center.

At the bend is one of the two memorials in the park to Rosalía de Castro; she sits stolidly in a chair, a plain-faced woman, with her back to the view, something which in life she would never have done. On the square pedestal below her is an inscription announcing that the memorial was underwritten by the Centro Gallego de La Habana, at whose hospital my father had stayed when he left Tampa to be cured. On another side of the pedestal is a bas-relief of a peasant couple looking like the souvenir dolls in the stores in Vigo, and under them, lines from one of her poems. An enormous spreading magnolia tree obscured the poem at that time of day, but I knew that it was one of the happier poems, written in Galician, from her first volume, *Cantares Gallegos,* a ballad in which the lovers, to be reunited one day, say farewell.

Rosalía was born in Santiago on February 24, 1837, the daughter of Doña Teresa de Castro and a still anonymous father, both of good families of Padron. Unlike the peasant women of the aldeas, Doña Teresa came to the city to have her child in secret, and stayed in a poor neighborhood of Santiago. When the time came, she sent her maid to the hospital with a note, and her name on that note must have counted for something, because the doctor left with the maid. At three in the morning, the two returned with the baby, and the priest on duty baptized the child in the chapel of the hospital, now magnificently preserved in all its grandeur on the ground floor of the luxury hotel, the Hostal de los Reyes Católicos.

There is no surname for Rosalía in her baptismal record, not even her mother's. The maid served as godmother and no mention is made of a godfather; the priest who officiated made the entry, as is the custom, and he noted that her parents were unknown and that the child was not placed in the orphanage but was taken away by the god-mother. This woman brought her up, and it is thought that Rosalía was not claimed by her mother until she was eight. She was unhappy, but her childhood and later life were not the hard life of the peasant; she received the minimal education that girls of such a milieu got in those days, she even went to Madrid to stay with relatives for a year when she was a young lady, and she married a re-spectable Galician writer. Yet she remained, as her three small volumes of great lyrics show, a daughter of the people.

Wherever you go in Galicia, Rosalía is with you: she seems to have created its consciousness and its landscape. And she is always a siren calling Galicians back home.

> Come back, for I swear to you
> that at the foot of every stream and fount
>   of clear water
> where once your face your face was shown
>   and in every old wall
> which lent you shade when you were young
>   and ceaselessly played . . .
>
> I swear and say to you
> that there are still mysterious spirits
> who call for you so hurt and loving,
> in so deep and sad an accent,
> they make our air unhappier to breathe . . .

I turned my back on her back, hating her for her siren call which had lost me my father, and stood in a columned arbor with a cement balustrade looking over the valley. A long series of steps with intermediate landings led down to formal gardens, a long and broad expanse of them in the shape of a half moon; on its borders, facing me, were a group of large institutional buildings all of the same design. No matter how I stared I could not make out whether one might be a charity home. Behind me sounded the murmur of the paseo, people occasionally laughed or called a child, and one couple who came to retrieve a small boy who had joined me at the arbor informed me that these were the buildings of the university. I asked if one were a convalescent home and they said no and pointed to one on the extreme right and told me it was the hospital of the university. "The new hospital," the husband said, and they walked off.

The light was almost entirely gone; I was facing east and it happened almost imperceptibly, as if a scrim had been dropped before the scene while I talked to the couple. It was all receding from me and I had not found the Asylum of the New Road. I kept my hands on that balustrade and it took all my strength to keep from calling, "Father! Father!" I wheeled and looked back, instead, at the bulk of Rosalía, and noticed that the branches of the ancient magnolia tree spread across the path between me and the monument and threw some shadow on the arbor: like the oak tree in the alley beyond our house in Tampa under whose branches I once called for Father.

I was five, we had come back from Havana, and it was Sunday. All the aunts and uncles and their children had gathered, and after lunch the children went to play baseball in the empty lots at the corner. I went too, but they would not let me play because I was too young and a bother. In a rage, I returned home, where the adults sat in the living room, and insisted that Mother call my sister out of the game. If I could not play, neither should she. Mother tried to explain but it made me angrier—the injustice of it!—and I screamed and circled the round table with the bowl of wax fruit in the center when my mother tried to catch me. I picked up a banana and yelled a word I had learned only that week: "Whore!"

It frightened me and I must have paused, for Uncle Antonio, a Galician from Lugo, caught me. He did not hit me. He dragged me through the living room, kitchen, back porch and yard, where he picked up a clothesline, and then tied me by the hands to the oak tree in the alley. I was to stay there until it was time for me to come inside and beg forgiveness. I was quiet for a while because the tears choked me and I did not want to ask anyone's forgiveness and I did not want any of the neighbors to see me there.

A black, fuzzy caterpillar fell on my arm, the kind we were used to pick up and play with, but my hands were tied and it crawled up my arm. I shook my arm but it did not fall off, and now that I had my breath I screamed. I meant to call Mother but instead I called Father, who was already back in Miamán tied to his death, and then I howled, just howled. I knew now in the Horseshoe Park that each howl, each cry which had so desolated me then, was a call for him: why had he left me, why was he not there to protect me?

During the war, when I was about to go overseas, I went to see Uncle Antonio to say goodbye. He and my aunt owned a little cigarstore in the East Bronx, and he walked up the El steps with me to say goodbye on the platform. "Do you remember," he said, "that I once punished you when you were a little boy?"

I said I did not remember.

"I did not hit you, I just tied you to a tree," he said. "You do not remember?"

I shook my head and it pleased him. "I did it," he said, "because it was what your father would have done and I wanted you not to miss a father's guidance. You know that your father and I were the same age and we both came from Galicia?"

At that time, my sister's and my feelings of being unprotected had long been displaced by the more disquieting one that we had somehow failed Father and that old woman to whom he came home for help. And although time helped us to accept the situation, we never forgot it, and it took the form with me, from the moment I met my cousins in Miamán, of asking why the old woman had stopped writing. The discovery that no one seemed to have cared much about my father, that the old woman had been content to live another thirteen years without letting us know, that my carnal cousin did not even know of our existence—these were the jagged little stones I brought back from our walk to Miamán, what became clear as the light disappeared in the Horseshoe Park.

While others enjoyed the paseo, I was the wailing, bereft boy of five again, and I knew in some subterranean, undefined way—despite the hard, sensible facts which explained it all—that it was I who had been abandoned. There was no Asylum of the New Road and my unremembered, mute, paralytic father had vanished into this air, become an atom of sorrow which made it sadder to breathe. And there was nothing to do, no one to be angry with—not even Uncle Antonio. I had to go about my business like Gustavo Andeiro, amputated of my lineage, with only a few creases and wrinkles to show how the wound had healed.

5

Along the waterfront of La Coruña, the ships nose up to the trees in the park, and all the activity of the port is a show for strollers in the alameda, guests in hotel lobbies, and middle-class idlers in the sidewalk cafés. When you walk by the water and look back at the slim peninsula of the city, you see that the town is all eyes: the glass-enclosed galerias of the old buildings look north and return a silvery gaze to all who look up, except during early morning and at sunset when they draw refracted colors out of the air and turn warm. But when it rains the soft rain of Galicia, they cry all day long.

North is Lugo where Uncle Antonio came from, a few miles beyond the other side of the fjordlike ria, and we might have visited it if Uncle Antonio had a relative there or had asked me to. But he had been back there with my aunt and their two boys right after the first world war and made his peace with it, and it no longer interested him. At least that was what I now made of our conversation on the El platform in the Bronx during the war; he had kept me there, as one train after the other came and went, until he told me the whole story.

"Like your father I lost my father when I was little and so I had to work all the time, and when I was twelve and soon to leave for Havana, I still did not know how to read and write properly," he said. "It was a worry to me, for although I knew I would have no trouble becoming an apprentice in a cigar factory in Havana, the time would come when I would need to read and write.

"Our farm was so close to town I could walk to it, and because I persisted my mother sent me to an evening class run by a young schoolmaster. I paid just like everyone else, but the other young fellows came from the better families and he paid little attention to me. I always sat at the back of the room where I could not see the board well and got only crumbs like a poor relative."

One day Uncle Antonio hurried through his chores and got to the school in time to take one of the front seats in the classroom. The boy who considered it his own asked him to move when he arrived, but Uncle Antonio would not, until the teacher came in and made him change to his old seat in the back of the room. "I did it but I grumbled all the way to my seat and afterwards too, for there I had to sit with the lightbulb's glare in my eyes. In a while I told the teacher I was sitting there under protest, that after all I paid just like the other students. Well, I finally got that teacher so mad that he slapped me hard on the face."

Uncle Antonio looked at me to see what I thought of that, and I shook my head and we waited for the subway train to rumble out of the station before he resumed his story. "I have never forgotten that slap. It does not matter how old I get to be, I shall never forget it. At the end of the class, I told Conde—that was his name and I shall not forget it either—that he had hit me because my father was dead and I therefore had no protector. And I went home that night and told my mother—she and my aunts used to sit together and knit—that I was not going back to the school, forgetting that it had been I who had insisted on going."

Uncle Antonio interrupted his story to point a moral: the experience had been good for him, since he was always on the alert from then on about injustices. This was an attitude which stood him in good stead in Havana, where all the apprentices were boarded in the attic of the factory. "For many were the abuses which we suffered there, such as fighting to get my own alcove with a permanent bed when my turn came and not having to set up a cot every night and take it apart in the morning. When I put away that cot in the morning and stacked it with the others, I might as well have been a zero, for I could not even point to a place and say, That is where I sleep.

"But let me not forget Conde," said Uncle Antonio. Seventeen years later, he had saved enough money to return, for he wanted to see the old woman before she died and to show her his wife and boys. "Every afternoon I used to drop by a tavern to see old friends and have a drink, for that is the way it is in Spain. I had seen Conde once or twice but I had never been in any gathering with him, until one day he was at the tavern when I was there. I said to the barman—Cuellar was his name—to serve a round of drinks on me. We were all having a good chat though I had not addressed one word to Conde, and when the barman came to Conde he paused just before he refilled his glass, as a matter of form, and looked at me. I said as casually as I could, No, I do not know the gentleman, though of course everyone knew I knew Conde, and in any case, in Spain when you treat at a bar you make no distinctions.

"Poor Cuellar, he pulled up the bottle so quickly that not a drop fell out, and to this day I wish I had watched Conde's face to see if it got as red as mine when he slapped me. But of course I went on talking to a friend and did not look at him, and he left soon after that very discomfited, or at least that is what the others told me. When he was gone, Cuellar said, Listen, just out of curiosity, why did you refuse to buy Conde a drink? I told them all the story and then someone bought another round and it was all worth waiting seventeen years for!"

Thinking about Uncle Antonio's story during my first reflective day at La Coruña—after sundown those dreamy galerías close their eyes and the city becomes very gay with the paseo time—it seemed to me that Uncle Antonio had repaid Galicia for its slap in the face, not just Conde. And I wished that was how I could feel about Santiago. Not that Uncle Antonio was not a sentimental Galician too: the mail had caught up with us in La Coruña and I had a letter from Mother telling me that Uncle Antonio, now seventy-eight, had just left by plane—"at his age"—to visit his only remaining brother in Buenos Aires. He had not seen him in sixty-five years, and I imagined him in Argentina now telling his brother how he got even with Conde.

It is a peculiarity of mine that happenings present themselves to me with proper endings, that they are not even happenings unless they have a rounded ending; and when the ending is not there and I cannot impose one on it, it makes me restless and unhappy. An unhappy ending has its satisfactions: a fulfillment despite the odds of human desires, so perfect and inevitable a formal pattern that it both displaces and creates a sense of justice. We spent five days in La Coruña and I found no ending I could impose on our trip to Miamán and Santiago.

There was no question that I had to go back to Santiago: I must look up my father's death record. If it turned out that he was buried in the churchyard at Miamán, I would of course have to go there. But I hoped I would not need to. Santiago yes, because it was beautiful . . . anyway, the records were there. By the time we returned, Paco, my cousin's son, would be off for his summer military training, and Luz and Gustavo spent all their time at El Gran Derby. I would not think about it, I'd see how I felt when I was there.

We had spent that last morning in Santiago, before coming to La Coruña, with Paco. We did the tour of the cathedral with a guide, and later we walked up and down the Calle del Franco in and out of the cafes frequented by the students with money. Paco had shown up at our hotel promptly at ten dressed in a gray suit, white shirt and tie, and although he was somewhat disappointed that we hired a guide for the cathedral and did not trust to him alone, his self-confidence revived with our praise of the things we saw, as if the great sculptures of the Gloria Portico in the cathedral were not Master Mateu's but Galicia's, and Rosalía de Castro's lyrics were his own. He was right, of course, but his identification came too easy, especially for a young man taking the three-year "social" course to prepare him for work in an *empresa,* a corporation.

He was now twenty-one and had already spent six years in the city of Santiago, for there were no real schools in Miamán to prepare him for the university, and his parents had to part from him and do without his help on the farm so that he could get an education. "I am very drawn to the countryside because of all my years in Miamán," he said, "but it is a romantic interest, I would not want to work there any more."

"It was very beautiful yesterday," my wife said.

"*It was the month of May,*" he recited, "*the month of love . . . the month of flowers.* I have not seen it all spring and I shall go tomorrow to say goodbye before I leave for the summer with my platoon."

We sat in a sidewalk cafe across from the College of Pharmacy, and studied the figures on the Renaissance portal of the building while he talked. I already knew that he had never heard of my father or of his father's cousins in America and that his knowledge of the architectural styles of the cathedral was imprecise; and the previous day's adventures returned to me insistently and beguilingly, making me forget his presence. I came to once and heard him talk proudly about Spain's exhibit at the World's Fair in New York as the jewel of the fair and let it pass, as I had often done with middle-class Spaniards, with just a nod. The next time I listened he was extolling Franco, his resistance to Hitler during the war, his peaceful statesmanship, the independent position he had gained for Spain. "There is no turmoil in Spain as in other places," he said, sure of our admiring interest.

I told him that I knew many Spaniards felt as he did, but that I had also met many who did not. "The impression you get of peace is mainly to be gotten from the newspapers," I said, "for they do not report the riots of the students in Madrid or the sympathy strikes of the universities in other cities. Do you know that last month three thousand Asturian miners marched into Mieres and attacked the police headquarters successfully enough to release their union leaders who had been jailed?"

"Some of the students here also talked of going on strike, but when the authorities let them know that strong measures would be taken, they gave up the idea," he said, and laughed, still expecting me to go along with him.

"I must tell you that outside of Spain people do not think of Franco the way you do," I said. "For all the friendly relations between our government and yours, most Americans do not like him. I do not know if you know that the great majority of Americans sympathized with the Republic during the civil war."

He was a nice young man and he would have liked to agree with anything I said, so that his face seemed to disintegrate with the desire to show interest and hide his shock.

"One thing more," I said, mercilessly. "In Tampa, all the Galicians and Asturians were very strongly on the side of the Republic. You would not have had a single friend there if you had been for Franco."

He brought his face under control, and he nodded and said politely, "I see."

I was ashamed of myself: all this was what I should have said to his uncle. "That is not to say there is nothing wrong with the United States or that the Americans do not like the Spanish people," I said, sounding like a pompous editorial writer.

Paco paused and then dared say what he was thinking: "There is a great deal of unrest in your country, I hear. There is all that trouble with the Negroes."

I remembered the old joke about the American visitor to Moscow: having listened at length to the glories of its subway, he pointed out that trains ran infrequently, only to have his guide reply, "But you have lynchings in the South!" I didn't laugh at Paco, I simply said, "Yes, things are very bad for the Negroes," and this puzzled him, for he expected that I would add, as Spaniards happy with the regime always do about its shortcomings, that we had plans to change all that.

So few students on the Calle del Franco greeted Paco
that I suspected he was seldom there, that it was a middle-
class scene he had yet to make. It was Paco who two or
three times called out to others, and immediately after
talked to us so animatedly that it seemed our presence
added to his social stature. We took him to lunch at the
Hostal, and he volunteered that he had never been inside.
"Few students," he said, lumping himself with all the
others, "can afford it." He acquitted himself well at the
table and enjoyed the elegant service; his qualms about
me, after our troublesome exchange, were wiped out by
the lunch: no one who could afford the Hostal, he must
have thought, can be all bad.

In La Coruña, for which Paco saw us off after that
lunch, our cafe faced the alameda and the harbor—if you
cannot find a cafe your first day in a Spanish city that you
can call your own, then you must leave that city immediately, for you will never feel at home—and one day there,
the very one when the waiter knew what to serve us without asking, we watched a stream of children cross the
park and head past our tables for the street beyond. They
were Scots, a whole shipload from Edinburgh on a ten-
day tour to Gibraltar, and in the Galician sunlight they
looked pale and undernourished. But they had the gaiety
and abandon of children just let out of school, and they
were torn between the desire to sit at the cafe and immediately order orange juice—the English in Spain are mad
for oranges the way New Yorkers in Miami are for
sunshine—or dash ahead to the shops.

Some of the larger shops knew of their coming and had

brought out tables to the sidewalk full of souvenirs: peasant dolls, miniature orreos, castanets. Rafael followed the children, and we sat alone at the cafe until a middle-aged couple from the Scottish ship joined us; La Coruña was their first stop, Vigo next, then Lisbon, Cadiz and Gibraltar. They were both teachers and we learned from them that the tour was very inexpensive, purposely so to make it possible for these working-class children. "We've warned them not to spend all their allowance here," the woman said. Just before lunch Rafael returned; he had spent the morning acting as interpreter at the souvenir counters, and the children straggling back to the ship for their lunch stopped to say hello and get more instructions from Rafael on how to hold the castanets.

"Did you have a good time?" my wife asked.

"It's been great fun!" a boy said, and one of the girls hugged herself and squealed.

There was not one dark, brown-eyed child on the ship and they were wearing their best clothes, but I was reminded of young Carlito in his patched pants in the yard at Miamán, his eyes full of nostalgia for the world we evoked. There he was: hanging back, watching, not saying a word, letting his eyes speak for him. I remembered, then, the day my father left Tampa. I was two and a half, and keeping an eye on my father; I jumped off the packed trunk in the living room and stood in the doorway of the bedroom where my father had just gone. My mother stood at the dresser; they opened and closed the drawers. "Socks, socks," my mother said. That was all I could remember: I was small, my head didn't reach the doorknob, they were tall, transparent presences.

Then I heard my cousin Viola's voice when I was eleven and the letter from Miamán had arrived saying he was dead: "You were always dragging after him and crying if he went out without you. Once you followed him to the corner and you were wearing a dirty undershirt and diapers, and he gave you his hand, poor man, and took you with him, he limping and you skipping for joy."

Rafael poked my hand with the straw from his drink. He poked again; I stare ahead when I'm thinking and he doesn't like it. "Stop it," he said.

"I was thinking about Rosalía de Castro," I said. "There's a line in one of her poems in which she talks about herself—*There she goes, there goes the madwoman dreaming*. People also called her *la llorona*—the big weeper."

"I bet you were thinking about her," my wife said.

The bus for Santiago is boarded on a sidewalk across from the rose garden in the alameda in La Coruña. Long before the porters started loading bundles and old suitcases in the small belly of the bus, people began saying goodbye. The different parties became one mass as the bus revved up, crying and laughing and standing under the windows, handkerchiefs knotted in their fists. A girl at a second-floor galeria at the corner opened the center panes; around her shoulders and head were bright geraniums in bloom. "I'm sorry," I said to my wife, "that we didn't bring Carlito with us to La Coruña. He's probably never been farther than Santiago."

"Santiago de Compostela!" my wife said, ready for another pilgrimage.

At the hotel desk in Santiago, they said, "Welcome, welcome!" I did not mention we were one day late and they were too polite to remind us. "The room with bath for you and your lady," the desk clerk said, dropping all pretense, now that we were old friends, that there was more than one so equipped to each floor, "and a small one across the hall for the young master." He handed us keys heavy and big enough for a Robert Louis Stevenson adventure and said, "La Coruña is very gay, isn't it? Still, Santiago has its charms."

We stood on our little balcony and looked at our street; the restoration work on the Romanesque church had progressed slightly, and the movie theater in one of the ancient buildings just beyond was opening for the first show. It was too late to catch a mass at the cathedral important enough to merit the singing of the Hymn to Saint James and the swinging of the botafumeiro; tomorrow morning, we'd make certain to catch it. A woman went by carrying an enormous bundle of groceries on her head, casually as Galician women do, and stopped to talk to another on whose head was a long flat wooden tray with sardines. In a moment, we said to one another, we'll go down to our cafe across from the Horseshoe Park and watch the paseo. Then the phone rang and the man at the desk downstairs told me there was a gentleman there to see me. "You see how at home we are," I said to my wife. "We're even getting phone calls."

It was Gustavo Andeiro; he stood at one end of the desk

wearing gray slacks, white shirt and tie, and an *americana*, which is what Spaniards call a sports jacket, and looking circumspect and determined not to be surprised by anything in the lobby. He shook hands, smiled at my exuberant greeting, and immediately began a speech which informed me that he had come to check if I were back from La Coruña. I interrupted him, took his arm and led him upstairs, and he had a difficult time keeping to his mission and still observing the furnishings, the polished banister of the staircase, the plants and flowers on the landing. "Padrino came here yesterday to ask for you," he said, "but they told him you were not back yet."

"Claudio came!"

Gustavo nodded soberly. "He would have come sooner," he said, and looked at me as if this behavior of Claudio Balan's surprised him too. "But he knew you were still in La Coruña." He stopped me by coming to a halt in the corridor before we reached our room. "He wants you to know that if you had gone to Madrid and were not to return he would have followed you there."

It was as important to me, suddenly, as it was for Gustavo to impart the message. "That is very amiable of him, but I had every intention of visiting him in Miamán," I said, and told myself that of course that was true.

I opened the door of the room, and before stepping in, he said, "I took the liberty of coming here to find out, as Padrino asked me to do, if you were coming to Miamán and when."

"Here is Gustavo!" I said to my wife. "He wants to know when we are going to Miamán again."

139

He looked at the beds and headboards and covers. We made him sit on an upholstered wing chair by the balcony, and he sat in it carefully, and primly brought his knees together. "Padrino wants to be sure when because he wants to have all the cousins at his house. He heard that you want to meet them all."

We said we would come Sunday but that we did not want him to go to so much trouble. By this time Gustavo had taken a good look at the dresser and mirrors, our suitcases and the stand for them, but he kept his mind on his business and said, "Then Sunday it is? For I must send the message to him." It was Friday afternoon and he could see I wondered how he would do it. "By the afternoon bus to Trazo," he added.

I apologized for having put him to the trouble of looking us up at the hotel and assured him we meant to drop by El Gran Derby the next day. I also told him how well he looked, how interesting La Coruña was but that Santiago was better, a rush of talk which I hoped would make him feel how happy I was about his and Claudio's attentions to us. I slowly came to a halt when I noticed his lack of responsiveness.

He had not finished his business. "I have made inquiries," he said as soon as I stopped, "about where your father stayed. A man who is a customer of mine at El Gran Derby has connections with the Asylum of the New Road—I used to also but I do not any more because it is very hard to collect from the sisters—and to do me a favor he spoke to the Directress. It says in their records that he died there in 1931 and that is all. I had thought, as I told you, that he was buried in the holy ground of the church at Miamán, but Padrino says no, that it must have been at the Santo Domingo cemetery here."

That was a long speech for him, and when he finished, he seemed to go over it in his mind to see if he had left anything out. "Yes?" I said to encourage him.

"You can find out at the *ayuntamiento* where he was buried," he said. "But it must have been Santo Domingo because that is where they were buried in those days."

"They" must be paupers, and I was so occupied with the thought that I did not answer.

"It is my belief, however, that the records at the Asylum must say more, for this customer who asked for me is, after all, not a person . . . of influence. And I believe that if you were to go you would find out more." He looked at his watch. "I shall go with you."

I put on my jacket, and he stood up. He pointed to the tall, old-fashioned clothes wardrobe. "It is disgraceful that for the money you must pay here they put such things in their rooms. I would not have it at my place." There was a slight smile on his face, as if he were happy he had had the courage to make the comment after all.

He led me to the Horseshoe Park, but instead of walking into the alameda he took a sidewalk along a street which sloped with the land, a street where the buildings were no longer old. Before we reached the bottom of the hill beneath the park, he stopped and asked, "Now, what was your father's name?" I told him and he nodded and we went on. The Asylum was a neat square building taking up about half a block. "At one time," Gustavo said, "it stood here by itself," and he gestured to the houses across the road and beyond the Asylum on the same side of the street to show what had been added.

I was not ready to go in and talk to the Directress yet, so I turned my back to the building before we reached the entrance and looked across the road; it was a lovely farming valley along which we had come on the bus from La Coruña, and it must have made a sweet view for my father to look at. When I turned around, I saw the sign on the stucco wall to one side of the entrance:

HERMANITAS

DE LOS

ANCIANOS DESAMPARADOS

RESIDENCIA

"Apóstol Santiago"

Little Sisters of Abandoned Old People, Apostle Saint James Home. I told myself that *desamparados* should in that context be translated as "needy," not "abandoned," and we walked up to the wooden double doors and knocked.

The porter talked to us in the neat, spare lobby, and pointed to dark inner doors to a chapel and said the Directress would be out as soon as mass was finished. Gustavo did not choose to tell him in detail what we wanted to ask the Directress, and I decided to let him be the one to handle the coming interview, for I had never spoken to a nun and felt strange being there. I could hear chanting from behind the closed doors to the chapel. I wondered how my father felt being taken care of by little sisters whose church he hated, and suddenly recalled, as I

turned the word *desamparados* over in my mind, how my
mother and aunts had cried when Aunt Lila and Uncle
Arturo announced that they were accepting the charity of
WPA. I heard Gustavo volunteer to the porter that I had
come from America and had inquiries, which were important to me, to make of the Directress. The porter's eyes
got a little larger and we looked at one another and
nodded.

The group which came out of the chapel was all
women, from young matrons to elderly ladies, all of them
full of chirping questions of the Directress. The Directress
was a young nun, used like a public personality to han-
dling groups, and each time she answered one of the
ladies she glanced aside, hoping to put an end to the question. During one aside she saw us and took a few steps
toward us and nodded.

"Señora," Gustavo began with just a suggestion of
deference, and she immediately placed him from his tone,
accent and lack of pious address. She did not change her
manner nor stop listening, but her replies lost the tone of
attempting to please and were instead efficient, equable,
unencouraging, like a good clerk's. The middle-class
ladies were not fooled by Gustavo's americana—they had
their own way of gauging his status—and they interrupted him without apologies. The Directress answered
them with just a touch of indulgence missing from her
manner with Gustavo, but she did not turn away from us,
and signified by the gaze she kept on Gustavo that she
was still listening to him.

When he finished, she said, "No, the gentleman who inquired has all the information. Our records only give the date of his death, if I remember correctly May of 1931, and no more."

She was pale and thin and businesslike and I decided she was a true mystic like that other good organizer, Saint Teresa. She looked at me as she finished her reply, but since we had not been introduced turned back to Gustavo. She knew that he would have to ruminate a moment before he could compose a question, and she waited quietly, just the movement of one hand over the other betraying that she hoped he would get to it soon. His questions always led to the same original reply from her, but when he said the man he was inquiring about was my father, she turned to me. "In those years," she said, "very simple records were kept. Now much more information would appear, but that is not to say that they overlooked the most essential, for the date of death is all you need to find out at the ayuntamiento just what the death certificate included and where he was buried."

I thanked her and was impatient to be off, for the middle-class ladies now watched me curiously and no longer interrupted.

"It is my opinion," said Gustavo, "that he was buried at Santo Domingo."

"Yes, that seems most logical for those days," said the Directress. "Unless other arrangements were made." She looked at me, then, as if saying someone like me would have done that. Then she asked her only question, the only gesture to prolong the interview: "Are you planning to transfer the remains?"

I had not thought of such a possibility, did not have the money for it, did not think myself someone whom such sentiments touched and, all in a rush, was both ashamed and surprised. And I reacted out of a taught response which skipped all the years of my adulthood and sprang from a maxim learned in childhood from the cigarmakers in Tampa: Get away quick from nuns and priests or they will get money out of you. "I do not know," I said, saying no to her unspoken question: Don't you want to repay retroactively the charity extended to your father years ago?

The young Directress turned back to Gustavo, as to someone she could understand, and reviewed with him the advisability of going to the ayuntamiento rather than the cemetery to check the facts. He agreed with her and thanked her, but I felt sure that Gustavo approved, out of the same motives as the Tampa cigarmakers, my having been so reserved about my plans. We walked up the hill to the Horseshoe Park quietly and at ease with one another.

And so we remained for the next hour while waiting for the driver of the bus which returned each evening after seven to Trazo with the workers it had brought to the city twelve hours earlier. Only once did he show the irritation with me that had made him say at our first meeting that he would not travel to the States as a tourist and, earlier that afternoon, that the clothes wardrobe in our hotel room was unfit for El Gran Derby. There was a modern cafe on high ground in the park overlooking the shabby side street where the driverless wreck of a bus was parked, and I insisted that we have a drink and wait at one of the tables of the cafe for the driver to show up. He gave in, but it was obvious that he was not one to pamper himself with refreshments between meals, even when he didn't have to pay for it.

Once we had ordered beer, however, he relaxed, but he put his foot down about having a plate of crisp-fried squid rings to chew on between sips, and I did not overrule him and order it anyway, as is proper to do with a protesting Castilian. Gustavo watched the young waiter critically as he poured the beer with a flourish, while seeming to ignore him at the same time, for he did not bother to return the waiter's smile and slight bow as he finished. Yet he was happy to be the object of service, and I found out that he had not been insensitive to what I had experienced at the Asylum of the New Road.

"It is not important where you are buried once you are dead," he said to me and leaned his head to one side, the way the cousins in Miamán did when they meant to be kind. "Not important at all where your father and my mother are buried."

"Well, having come this far and having promised my mother . . ." I said.

"That goes without question," Gustavo said, man to man. "And if you cannot get satisfaction at the ayuntamiento tomorrow, this man I know who asked at the Asylum will be happy to inquire. Padrino too is certain we can find out, do not worry."

I said I planned to go tomorrow morning, and we

sipped the beer and I told him how beautiful I thought the Horseshoe Park was.

He did not follow my gaze to the awesome trees along the alameda: it was not his park, he never joined the paseo there, or anywhere. He looked down at the table and closed and opened his fist, a characteristic gesture when about to speak from the heart. "I would give anything—anything!—to have my mother with me today. It would be worth everything to me—the years in Venezuela, everything."

I stared at him; he had surprised me. I did what Spanish men do when they agree or sympathize with one another: I leaned over and tapped him on the shoulder.

He looked up with his head to one side and smiled just a little. "Life is strange," he said.

I said yes, life is strange.

"You know, nowadays families cannot disappear, that is what I think," he said, and I knew that this was something he and Luz had discussed together and perhaps also with some of their friends at El Gran Derby; and they must have talked about it with Claudio Balan when he came to Santiago the previous day on the workers' bus from Trazo to look for us—while I was in La Coruña thinking badly of them. "Your children and my children would have found each other if they had cared, that is what I think."

He saw the driver then and got up, his momentary softness left behind at that unaccustomed cafe, and I followed him down to the side street. He told the driver to have his brother informed that their cousin was coming on Sunday, and the man looked over Gustavo's shoulder at me and touched a hand to his cap. I stepped forward, gave him my hand, said my name and told him I was his servant; and he said he was Eliseo Castro and he was there to serve me. Gustavo was very pleased by this exchange and pleased, too, I had the feeling, that he had carried through his brother's bidding; and when he left me at the polished double doors of the hotel lobby, it seemed plain that he was proud his meager lineage had expanded to include me.

This good feeling of acceptance stayed with me until the next morning, and at breakfast I first realized how childish and vain this response was: it was they who were supplying me with a lineage which I missed, I who should feel proud to have all these cousins. Coming out of the dining room that morning, I saw one of them—the little hunchback Asuncion—standing next to the double doors where Gustavo had left me. She looked tinier than in the yard at Miamán. "Here I am, Pepe!" she shrieked. "I came to see you!"

She wore her kerchief, a brown pleated wool skirt, a sweater over a plain blouse, and carried a woven basket like the workmen in the city. "I had to come to see the dentist and I said to myself I wonder what my cousin Pepe is doing?"

I bent down to kiss her cheek, and I saw her look triumphantly at the desk. In the same loud voice, she said, "They told me you were having breakfast."

"Why didn't you come in?" my wife asked, and I translated.

Asuncion shrugged her shoulders. "It was better that I waited for you," she said, and took my wife's hand and walked upstairs with her, looking like a strange waif my wife had picked up. I was to see the two of them walking like that during the day and each time it was to be as funny and painful a sight; the astonished looks of the men at the hotel desk were to be duplicated in the stares of passers-by.

We led her to the same upholstered chair in which Gustavo had sat, and it took her a while to settle in, first pulling up her pleated skirt to her waist before she lowered herself into it, like a New York lady who owns only one mink coat. Underneath she wore a silk slip with a wide lace fringe, and she stroked it and said to my wife, "It is a gift from Cousin Esperanza who brought it from Havana."

She already knew that we were going to Miamán the next day, and she said that they too were going to be at Claudio Balan's house. "Oh, Claudio is such a good man," she exclaimed, still in a voice tuned to the open spaces of Miamán. "He cannot wait to see you. He said that he would have followed you to Madrid if you had not returned from La Coruña."

I volunteered to go with her to the dentist, and she informed me that she had come to the city early with the workers' bus and had already been to the dentist. Now, she had only a few errands to do and then she would be free, so I said I would go with her. But my wife wanted her to sit a while and rest, and asked Asuncion if she always had to make a trip to Santiago to go to the dentist.

"*I* do," she said, and then felt she had been too critical of the others in Miamán. "There is no dentist nearer and people cannot leave their work just because their teeth hurt. And you know, we are a little foolish in Miamán. Look what happened to me when I had the accident."

She was twenty-three, six months after she had given birth to Carlito, and she was sitting on the wagon piled high with the yellow-flowering bush. "We had been cutting all afternoon and I liked sitting up there on top of all those branches, just resting on the way home." A wheel slipped into a deep rut and she fell off the wagon on her back. "If such a thing happened to a child of mine, you think I would not take her to a doctor?" She lay in bed a few days, in terrible pain, then began to hobble about when the bones began to mend. "But I was never out of pain and I have looked this way since. You see why I say we are a little foolish in the aldea?

"Well, a short time ago there was a doctor in Trazo. Not exactly a doctor but a man who knew a lot about bones. He was not a doctor but he was very knowing. He looked at me and he said that I had broken my back and the bones had grown together again but all wrong. To fix me he would have to break them all again and he said the pain from that would be very terrible. I do not think my heart would take it."

She looked at each one of us and then smiled. "As soon as I put an ounce more than twenty-five pounds on my head my back begins to hurt. And Pepe, you know us Galician women, we do not use our heads to think but to carry things. Ana Feijoo carries more than a hundred pounds on her head as if it were nothing. And me, I am good for nothing and I look one hundred years old."

I had never been called Pepe, which is the equivalent of Joe for Joseph, and Asuncion not only initiated it that day but she never had to be told to call me *tu*. Yet she would not let me carry her basket for her because it would not look right. I had, it seems, been too quick for her in the lobby and picked the basket up before she did, but now that we were going to be out in the street, it would be too shameful for me to carry the basket and not she. I held the basket in my hand, she begged, I said no, and we compromised by leaving it in the room, once she made certain that my wife and Rafael would be there all the time to watch it.

"Once I do these errands," she said softly, as if to herself, "I am free for the whole day."

We told her we hoped she would spend it with us.

"I do not even have to return on the bus," she said. "They do not need me in the aldea until tomorrow."

I said we would take a room for her in the hotel, and she shrieked, "No!"

"Do you prefer to stay at El Gran Derby?" I asked.

"No, I shall stay with a friend who lives here in Santiago. I only need to tell her and it will be all right." She looked down at the floor, on the verge of a confession. "Would you believe it, I have never been to El Gran Derby. I did not even go to their wedding." I said nothing, but she explained: "I do not know what it is, but Gustavo does not have the character of Claudio, there is not that openness about him."

Unerringly she took turns in the street which immediately got us out of the business and middle-class section of the city, and during the next two or three errands we made, she managed never to leave the poor streets of the city. "Carlito showed me the money you gave him, after you left," she said, as soon as we were outside. "He said, Look how much money Uncle Pepe gave me, Mother, and I said it was all right because, after all, it was not as much to you as it is to us."

First we went to a small wine merchant from whom she was going to order a barrel of red Galician wine for the house, and before we got there she told me that she also wanted to buy something each for Carlito and Consuelito, her little girl. My wife had already bought gifts for each person she had met in Miamán, so I did not feel that I should take her statement as a hint to me; rather, I felt like telling her that since she was going to return to Miamán in the taxi with us, she should forget about getting the children something and so spare herself the expense. Especially since she said that they had been very hard hit that week: one of the oxen had been sick and they had to take it to a veterinarian in the town by the highway and the inoculations had cost a fortune.

"Carlos was very depressed by the ox being sick," she said, "but what can one do, the money has to be spent."

At the wine merchant's—a poor place with dank interiors—she told the surprised owner that the last barrel had not been so good.

"Why, what was wrong with it?" he said.

"I cannot say exactly," she answered in her soft voice,

"but it was not as good. Did anyone report to you that it was a little sour?"

"No," said the merchant, "there was not a single complaint about that shipment."

"So what are you going to give us this time?" she said. He gave her some to taste. "Do you think this is good?" she asked.

"Woman, of course I think so," he said.

"I wanted your opinion," she said, "because I know nothing about these things and I have to tell them at home."

The man never lost his humor, not even when she insisted on looking at the particular barrel he was going to deliver to the workers' bus. They would drop it off at Trazo and from there Carlos would cart it on a wagon to Miamán. She studied the barrel for distinguishing marks. "How will I recognize it?" she asked worriedly. "It is the same as the one I tasted?"

"I can open it and let you taste it too," he said, "but you would not want that."

She thought about it a long time. "Make a scratch on it so there is no mixup," she said finally. "It costs so much money that one cannot make a mistake." She turned to me apologetically: "You know how it is when you are poor, Pepe, you cannot afford to make a mistake."

When she had said yes, and gone over in great detail how he would deliver the barrel, at what hour that day, where on the bus he would tie it, and how Carlos, now that she was staying overnight in Santiago, would know which was theirs—when she had done all this, I took out some money and told the man I was paying. The man said Carlos always paid when he came to town and settled accounts with him, but I insisted and he took the money.

Asuncion said, "Oh Pepe, there is no need for you to do that." But I could see that she was pleased, and she added, "Besides, I still have to get a bottle of sweet wine —for Ana Feijoo."

I told the man to charge for the bottle too, and Asuncion repeated, "Oh Pepe, there is no need for you to do that."

Outside, she told me that now she had to buy a kerchief for Ana Feijoo, one with a little color in it, for Ana was coming out of mourning for her brother after thirty-five months. "That long?" I said, and she looked at me blankly. She selected it at a stand in the public market, and she made them unfold every kerchief they had. The nicer ones she said were too expensive, but I told her I planned to pay for it. "Oh Pepe, there is no need," she said, and she picked one of those with a little blue in it. While I paid, she kept darting looks at the other stands. "Do you think," she said, "I should get something for Carlito and Consuelito now?"

I told her there would be other opportunities during the day and that perhaps she should not bother at all since my wife was bringing them something tomorrow. I was anxious to get to the ayuntamiento that morning, fearing it might be closed in the afternoon since it was Saturday, and the errands had already taken longer than I had expected. She listened to me without changing expression but gave me a quick, direct look when I mentioned the gifts for Carlito and Consuelito. There was just one more thing, then, she must do: go to the bus and tell the driver about the barrel being delivered.

On our way, she suddenly said, "My father felt so foolish the other day not remembering everything about your father. After you left, he remembered that it was he who had gone to Cuba with him when they were both thirteen. His memory is not so good, but he was in Havana with your father at the factory and you know how he is, so good, so innocent, not a live one like your father, so your father got the job and he had to come back."

I remembered how she had thrust the hard piece of cornbread in my hands when we sat at their table in Miamán, and she looked away now, as she always did after she had said something bold, and I saw her hump. She must feel that the whole world should make amends, and so in another block I had forgotten this new thrust of hers. Trusting to her harsher view of things, I said, "I cannot understand, Asuncion, why my grandmother stopped writing after Aunt Remedio died. We could have helped her then and she would not have had such a hard time raising the boys by herself."

We were walking single file on a narrow sidewalk, and she turned back to answer. "They are fools in the aldea!" she shrieked. "Do you know why she stopped writing? She stopped writing because she was afraid that your mother and her two little children would come to live with her and she would have three more burdens to support!"

I stopped and put one hand against the solid granite wall of the building for support. We were abandoned, I said to myself, I was right to feel that we had been abandoned. But I saw the fear in Asuncion's face that she had gone too far, and it took me only a moment to see the dreadful humor of it. I shook my head and we walked to the rickety bus in silence.

Eliseo Castro, the bus driver, acted like an old friend this time, and since he knew Asuncion well, he gave her every assurance that the barrel would not fall off, that he would not fail to give her brother Carlos all her messages, that she might, in fact, take it for granted that the barrel of wine was already at home in Miamán. I was impatient; it was near eleven; I was more intent than ever on finding out what the death records at the ayuntamiento had to say about my father.

As soon as we walked away, Asuncion stopped again. "Oh Pepe, I am worried," she said. "That bus goes back full of young men and you know how young men are—what if they siphon off some wine from the barrel during the ride?"

I saved the driver's having to reassure her about this particular worry, and, now that I knew where I was, led Asuncion past the entrance to the Horseshoe Park, through the lively streets with restaurants, cafes and shops. A different kind of impatience dogged her: to make her plea for purchases of all kinds before we joined my wife again. "Oh, Carlito needs a wrist watch!" she exclaimed, inflamed by the sights in the shop windows. "Let me look at these shoes a moment. Consuelito would love a pair of little white sandals."

Getting to the hotel became a tug of war, and I excused

my resistance to her suggestions by telling myself they were wildly impractical: Carlito needed unpatched clothes, and white, open-work sandals would disintegrate in the muddy lanes of Miamán. Yet my wife had already bought for Consuelito, with my approval, a large doll whose long-lashed eyes opened and closed and which, when moved from a cradled position, squeaked, "Mama! Mama!" I told myself that I would give Carlito himself enough money to buy something he needed. As we neared the corner of our street, Asuncion made her last attempt: "Look, Pepe, a television set!" I laughed, and because it startled her, I explained that it was a new gas range with a look-through oven.

On the way to the ayuntamiento, I saw her holding my wife's hand and carrying the woven basket. I had lost the argument to carry the basket and we had walked the four long blocks to the magnificent Plaza del Obradoiro without her making any suggestions or even hints of things I could buy. True, we had only enough money to take us back to the States, but I knew then, in the rush of pity that seeing Asuncion at a distance always excited, that I resisted her because of what she had, I thought, perversely revealed about my grandmother. Yet however obvious her reasons, she spoke the truth: out of that awkward little form abrasive, shocking little truths stuck out.

In one wing of the palace which housed the city administration was the small office where death records were kept, as disarranged and inefficient-looking as an old-fashioned scholar's study. But the man there, his eyes wide with interest at our mission, reached unhesitatingly

for the bound book of May 1931. He found the page. "The
death was on May 26," he said, and kept on reading; I
watched his hand move down the page and thought, yes,
he died, a reassuring statistic.

The man lifted the book to the counter and turned it
toward me, and I read each line on the form until I got
to the one which said he died of "general paralysis." I said
it aloud and only my wife understood; the man and
Asuncion seemed to think it was a reasonable illness. I
looked quickly at the form again and saw that it did not
say where he was buried, and the man informed me that
another office in the same building would tell me. He
typed out Father's name and the date of his death on a
blue slip of scratch paper and handed it to me, so that I
would not forget it by the time I found the other office.
Then before he took the book away he pointed to one of
the entries without a word, as if to get my attention only.
It was one at the end of the same line which gave his
mother's and father's name, and it said—I read it for a
long time—that Father was a "bachelor."

We went down the stairs to the wide gallery along the
street and climbed up again into another wing of the
enormous building. This time we were guided to a bigger
and lighter room and we had to wait while someone
else finished some inquiries. There was hardly any room
between the door and the railing, but Asuncion squeezed
in ahead of my wife. "You know why it said that he was
a bachelor?" she said in the soft voice I had come to mis-
trust. "It is because he was the object of charity and Aunt

Dolores probably did not want to give them too much information."

In this office they had to look in two books. One to find the number of the plot where he had been buried, the other to see whether "the remains" were still there. A line was drawn across the page for that plot number, and underneath a new person's name was entered with a 1949 date. "The remains were raised," the man said, looked at me, and explained that whatever was dug up was then put into a common grave with others. "And there is no record for that," he added.

I didn't know why but I gave him the blue slip from the first office and asked him to write on it the new information he had just told me. Going down the stairs I read it: he had written that Father was buried in the Municipal Catholic Cemetery of Santo Domingo in the city of Santiago de Compostela on June 4, 1931. A full nine days after he died. What happened during those nine days? Did medical students at the university learn their anatomy from him? Quite arbitrarily I decided that had not happened, and I turned the blue scrap paper over and saw that it was a throwaway announcing the performance by the College of Philosophy drama group of three one-act plays by Bertolt Brecht. I was glad I had asked them to type the information on it and I folded it into my wallet, the only headstone my father has. It pleased me and would have pleased Brecht: a harsh little tale of how the poor survive.

At the bottom of the stairs, we looked across the sunlit

square at the cathedral and decided to join the day's pilgrims at another high mass. "Well," said Asuncion, glad to start on her sightseeing in Santiago, "all the problems you had are now resolved."

6

When we walked into El Gran Derby that Saturday afternoon, little Asuncion became quite meek, and so I was glad to find out that Gustavo was coming with us Sunday morning in the taxi to Miamán: it ensured Asuncion's good behavior. Gustavo did not ask me if he could come, he simply stated it: he treated me like family. And when Asuncion said she was spending the night at the home of a friend in Santiago, Luz said in a hurt tone, "You mean you are not staying here?—how can that be!" Asuncion looked down and gave in. Luz glanced at me and shook her head, taking it for granted that like a good member of the family I knew what a problem Asuncion and her taunts were.

We had already spent eight hours with Asuncion by the time we were ready to leave El Gran Derby, and although she must have been eager to tell Luz and anyone who would listen the scandalous story she had learned about us at lunch, she still insisted on going with us, at least until nine o'clock when she was going to have dinner at El Gran Derby. As a kind of respite, we decided to spend the intervening time at a movie, and we went to one starring Jerry Lewis; we had no choice because it was the only film in Santiago at which, according to the obligatory rating of the Church, children were permitted. No matter, it would be a refuge.

We bought orchestra seats, and after looking about at the other ladies who filled the theater, Asuncion surreptitiously lowered her skirt and sat on it. During the day she had picked up other city manners: in the dining room of the hotel, where we had had lunch, she began to experiment with lowering her voice once she noticed that the astonished waiters responded to her in what was almost a whisper. But she was not consistent and there were private bits of family gossip which reached the ears of the entire dining room.

On religion she spoke in a low tone. She asked me if we were not Catholics, for we had not knelt at all during the mass at the cathedral, and I told her that we did not practice any religion and that my family in Florida were not churchgoers. In the cathedral Asuncion had followed the mass in her own way and had frequently stood when the others knelt, but we may have simply confused her by our unchanging stance. "Well, we have to go to at least one mass a year," she said, and looked at the next table to make sure they could not hear. "Or they throw you out of the parish. If you do not like to live like us, go somewhere else, that is what they would say to you."

"Tell me," I asked, hoping I had perhaps misunderstood, "were my cousin Claudio Balan and your brother Carlos really in the war?"

"Oh yes," she said. "They were in the Volunteers of Galicia."

"They volunteered!" I exclaimed, speaking in a louder voice than I meant to.

And she brought one hand to her head and shrieked, "Volunteer! They went the way you pull hair from your head!" And she pulled at her own to show me.

As soon as the waiter brought us our first course—even in a second-class hotel the midday meal in Spain has at least four courses—I noticed that after serving my wife, he served me and Rafael, leaving Asuncion for last. I took my plate and placed it in front of Asuncion while the waiter was serving Rafael, but the waiter did not take my hint; we went through the same maneuver on the second course, and I gave up after that. It seemed to confuse Asuncion, for one, and I was afraid she might think that I was passing her my plate because I hoped for a better portion.

She apologized for leaving most of the mussels in the vinaigrette sauce. "I do not like shellfish," she said. "We are not used to them in the aldea. We are a little foolish . . . You know, Pepe, I have been thinking about Aunt Dolores not writing to your mother and I think it must have been because she could not write after my uncle died and also it may have been that your mother's letters did not reach her. They sometimes get lost, letters do."

I took it that she had regretted her morning's outburst, and did not answer. I asked her about my cousin Claudio Balan, to change the subject. "Oh, Claudio, he is such a good man," she said. "He was such a handsome young man, it is a miracle he married, for he was the father of three children before he seriously courted Isabel and *she* was already far gone too when he married her . . . but her family had lands and that kind of reason for marriage exists in Miamán too, I want you to know.

"One of Claudio's children was by the daughter of the man who got his mother pregnant with Gustavo. So Claudio got his own back, he is no fool. It was a boy and he died when he was eleven. He was running in the house and turned over the pots of boiling water on himself. He only lasted two days.

"I cannot complain about my father," she said in a pious voice, as if changing the subject to please me. "He has always been good to me and never scolded me, even when he has had reason to. And he is such a good man, never cried over spilt milk, such as his lack of success in Havana when he was young."

Then, seeing she had not yet pleased me, she asked about our two older children in the States. There had never been an opportunity before to explain that the older children were my stepchildren, and I did so now. She looked quickly at my wife, and said to me, "You mean *you* were married before?"

I said they were my wife's children by her first marriage.

She was so shocked that she spoke in an aghast whisper. "Oh Pepe, do not say that! How could you have done such a thing? No Galician man ever would!"

I said that customs in other countries were different, that men and women divorced and then married again. "You sound," I said, "as if a Galician would not even marry a widow."

"Oh no!" she said. "A woman who has had a child cannot hope to marry again. I know I never could marry. And yet you . . ." She looked at my wife and said, "I know she cannot understand me or I would not be saying this in front of her. Oh Pepe, I cannot believe it!" She looked at my wife again. "I know, it was because you loved her, because she is so beautiful—you must have preferred her above all other women!"

"Exactly," I said.

When we left the dining room, as when we left the movie theater that evening, she took my wife's hand and looked at her with awe. But she never brought up the subject again, although after the movie we left my wife and son at the hotel and we were alone on the way to El Gran Derby. She dashed into a grocery store which was still open to buy just one item, but she was carried away again when she saw me take out money and bought several more.

When we showed up in the taxi at El Gran Derby on Sunday morning, Asuncion hardly greeted us, and I could tell by the first glance Gustavo and Luz both gave my wife that Asuncion had told them about the stepchildren. Asuncion feels guilty, I told myself, and that is why she is trying to be unobtrusive; but after a while I realized that in their presence she went back to being the unfortunate woman from the aldea: her holiday was over. Gustavo brought his little daughter with him, and Luz stayed in Santiago to take care of the restaurant. She gave my wife a special embrace when we all left—though my wife was unaware of it—as if to say she did not care about Asuncion's gossip, and Gustavo was courteous and deferential with my wife. I stopped feeling on the defensive.

The six of us filled the taxi and the packages we had all brought filled the trunk. Gustavo carried several things, one of them a large sponge cake; they had ordered it baked in a Santiago bakery, but Isabel, Claudio's wife, had sent fresh eggs from the aldea for it. It was a gala day, I could see, and the morning was as lovely as the first time we left for Miamán. Only the taxi driver was unhappy: Gustavo was making him take an unpaved country road to the heights of Miamán—"Man," the driver said to him, "it will kill my tires!"—and leave us close to the houses near the church.

Gustavo did not argue with the driver; he simply directed him, and there was that about his tone which said, I know you are overcharging my cousin and I expect you to earn the money. After a while, even the driver fell into the mood of the outing, and talked about the beauty of the countryside. The road was level in the main but full of sharp pebbles, and the driver had to go slowly so that they would not fly up and hit the car; we went through open fields, forests, two or three aldeas, until finally, on an open height, Gustavo told the driver to stop. We got out and took the packages which were for my cousin Claudio's house from the trunk, and Gustavo and his little daughter remained there. The rest of us went on in the taxi until suddenly the landscape became familiar: on a level with us was the church steeple and below was the field of corn seedlings and the huddled houses we had seen the first day.

At Carlos Andeiro's house everyone was waiting for us, except Ana Feijoo, who was still at mass, the one person in the family who went to church on Sundays. When she came, she looked at each gift my wife had brought and crossed herself. For Asuncion's girl we had brought the large doll, and little Consuelito hugged it to herself and then sat it on a chair. When we were about to leave for my cousin Claudio's home, a short, rosy-cheeked man came in, and Asuncion introduced him as Consuelito's godfather; he had Consuelito's coloring and eyes and rosebud mouth and he smiled at me as if saying, Yes, I am her father. He took the doll in his arms and watched it close its eyes. "What a marvel!" he said, and carefully put it in Consuelito's arms again.

Everyone wore his best clothes: Ana Feijoo still all in black but with a silk apron and kerchief; Carlos Andeiro in a jacket, though it did not match his pants and his shirt was collarless and tieless; the old man in those same patched, clean Sunday clothes; Jose Sabell in an unmatched jacket too, but looking less cadaverous because he had shaved. These four would walk to Nodar with us across the cornfield, for Asuncion was to come later, the old woman could not walk the distance and must stay home, and Carlito in unpatched blue pants was sent to the next aldea to represent the family at a wedding which they could not attend because of our coming.

Carlos Andeiro and Jose Sabell walked ahead with me, and in the field of corn seedlings I asked them if corn didn't more or less grow by itself. "Well, right now at this stage," said Carlos, "we have to go through each row and when there are two or three growing together—like this —we pull out the weaker ones and give the healthy one space to grow." He pulled up one short plant to demonstrate.

"Do they grow corn in your country?" Jose Sabell asked.

I said yes, but I did not tell him that the fields of corn in the Midwest grow for miles: it would not have been polite. I looked up toward the wooded hill, as on the first day, and asked Carlos Andeiro if he had explained to my cousin Claudio that I had not known that first day, until we were on our way to the taxi on the highway, that his home was so near.

"That evening as soon as we finished in the fields," Carlos said, "I went to his house and told him you had been here and that you were coming back and wanted to meet all your cousins. So it shall be, said Claudio, and he was on fire with the desire to meet you. He said that if necessary he would follow you all the way to Madrid."

"He is a good man, Claudio?" I said.

Jose Sabell and Carlos both stopped to give what they had to say proper stress. "A fine man," said one. And the other, "A very good man who has pulled ahead by working very hard."

"I am going to ask you a favor," I said. "Will you show me the house where my father was born?"

They laughed. "Of course. It is on the way there."

I called back to my wife in English that we would see my father's home, and she and the others caught up with us at the end of the field. Ana Feijoo crossed herself and tears came to her eyes.

"After you left," Carlos Andeiro said to me, "we were all wondering how it is that you understand Galician so well."

I explained that I knew a little French and Italian and those plus the Castilian helped me with the Galician. Carlos nodded, very impressed, and I heard Jose Sabell comment to Ana Feijoo and the old man behind me, "What is Galician to a man who is master of so many languages!"

We started up the lane through the eucalyptus and pine forest, and I tried to explain to Jose Sabell and Carlos that I was not master of many languages and that Galician was a fine language, that I wanted very much to learn it well if only because of Rosalía de Castro. "Look at that!" said Jose Sabell. "He has heard of Rosalía de Castro!"

"So I shall meet more cousins?" I said, to change the subject.

"Oh, there are more Andeiros and the Fragas and the Lopezes," said Carlos. "We are a large family and all the

169

older ones are probably right now at Claudio's waiting to meet you."

"But we shall stop to look at my father's house first," I said, and they assured me it was my day to command.

When the lane left the trees and houses appeared ahead, Carlos turned back to see where the others were. They had fallen behind, but he nevertheless lowered his voice and said in a confiding tone, "At Claudio's you will also meet Amparo Noceda."

"A cousin?" I asked, and knew in a way I cannot explain that I should stop for Carlos' answer.

We were close together but he took a step further toward me and put an arm around my shoulders. Jose Sabell moved closer and put a hand on my elbow. "Amparo Noceda was your father's woman the last time he returned to Miamán," said Carlos in a voice, low and loving, which said, We are men, we are cousins, there is no shame.

Their faces were close to mine, waiting for my response. I looked from one to the other and tried to shut out the resplendent sun in the fields beyond, reflected by the sharp stones and smooth leaves. Their faces held their expressions for an interminable moment, but when Jose Sabell's thin cheeks stretched into a smile and Carlos' hand patted my shoulder, I knew I must have smiled. "I am glad," I said. "I am glad for my father."

"Amparo Noceda is a fine person," said Jose Sabell, and I felt he was correcting me. "A good woman. She helped your grandmother take care of him and then later she stayed with your grandmother and worked her lands, especially when the Movement took Claudio away and Gustavo Andeiro was just a young boy."

Of all the things I could have thought, my mind chose to remember Gustavo Andeiro, the first day at El Gran Derby, talking about his madrina. "Is she Gustavo Andeiro's madrina?" I asked.

"Yes!" said Carlos, surprised that I knew, and I didn't want to explain that, except for his brother Claudio, she was the only person in Miamán Gustavo Andeiro referred to with love.

"I wanted to tell you," Carlos explained, "before you met her."

"And I thank you," I said. "I am grateful to you. And to her."

Carlos kept his arm on my shoulder and Jose Sabell put his around my waist, and we walked up the lane with our arms around one another like drunks leaving a bar at closing time, full of the good feelings that confidences bring.

At the first little cave of a house we came to on the lane, Carlos stopped and said, "That is where your father was born."

It was tiny and hugged the ground, its stones were weathered and black-brown with age; weeds and wild flowers, a tiny blue one like a delicate clover, grew in its interstices; and an underground stream surfaced in the small yard between it and the lane and left puddles in the grass. Its one window was on the side which faced the lane, a little square now boarded up, an eye shut to the world, and the sloping roof which made an open shed for the door was just beyond, to the side of the one-room house. The door was closed, there was no haystack in the yard, no wagon with cut bushes in the roofed shed: the little house seemed to be returning to the soil.

"It is not lived in any more," said Jose Sabell. "It is used as a storehouse."

We waited for the women and the old man and my son to catch up with us. Then we stood there and looked at it. In Alicante, on the Mediterranean shore, where the tourist apartment buildings are mushrooming, we had come across the ruins of houses of a Roman city—or was it Carthaginian or Phoenician?—uncovered by the new builders; and we had looked close at them, as we were doing now, trying to figure out what the day-to-day lives of the people who once inhabited them were like. There were no clues in Alicante, but here we had only to walk up the lane and see the barefoot children, the women leading the oxen home, looking at us with startled eyes, to know what it was like. A miniature Principal House of the Andeiros: inside was a corner, no doubt, under the chimney where the black pots hung over the open fire, a trestle table, two benches, a corner with straw mattresses, and a corner behind a partition where, if they were lucky, an ox and a cow had slept.

It must have been known in Nodar that we were coming to Claudio's house, for as we climbed the lane people came out to watch us go by. Carlos and Jose Sabell called out greetings to them, but did not stop to introduce us, and I had so much to think about and so many puddles and little mounds of dung to watch out for that the walk

172

from my father's home in Fuenfría to Nodar seemed like a fast ride in a car past a city block: short and blurred. Carlos turned into the door of one of the low houses, and announced that we were at Claudio's tavern.

Inside were barrels of wine and a low wooden counter behind which Gustavo Andeiro was serving some boys and two men. He filled their empty bottles with wine and made a note of the purchase, and he waited until he had finished with the men before he acknowledged our presence. His brother Claudio, he said, had gone to bring the cows from the field and would soon be there. "You are to wait here," he said.

His serious, withdrawn manner no longer fooled me. "What kind of a day off is this?" I said. "You might as well have stayed at El Gran Derby."

That sally was considered quite a witticism, and Gustavo Andeiro grinned but did not stop waiting on customers. The customers stayed to watch and listen, and Gustavo took out a broom when he had finished with them and began to sweep the dirt floor. There were no chairs in the tavern, only a bench and table and some piled-up boxes, and they were still trying to convince me to sit with my wife on the bench when I noticed an elderly woman standing just inside the door, quietly watching. She wore a blue skirt down to her ankles, a long-sleeved man's shirt of a striped print, and a kerchief of the same material as her skirt. She had the straight-shouldered posture of Galician women, and although she smiled and looked directly at me, she made no claim for attention, seeming only a shy observer.

Carlos Andeiro touched my elbow. "There is Amparo Noceda," he said, and waved a hand at her.

"Amparo Noceda!" I said and went toward her. She held out her hand and looked down. I took her hand and then embraced her and was surprised that for all her ruddy complexion, her strong, large face and straight body, she felt so slight and up close was so small. I kissed her on her cheek, and she looked up at me smiling, her eyes full of tears.

I kept her hand in mine and she struggled to say something but did not manage it. I had the feeling that everyone in the tavern was talking and exclaiming, but when I turned to introduce her to my wife and son, I saw that everyone was quietly watching. "Come," I said to her, "I want to take your picture," and led her outside to the lane.

No one followed us, not even the curious children. I embraced her again and she simply smiled and nodded and let the tears roll down her cheeks. "You stay there," I said, and stepped back. She straightened her shoulders and looked at me quizzically. Through the viewer I noticed the glint of light on her shirt; it came from a small safety pin which held her shirt together where a button had fallen off.

When I took her hand again, she first spoke. "You are very tall," she said, and her voice was low and husky like an old actress's.

"Amparo, do you remember my father?" I said.

"Sir?"

"No, not sir," I said, and then repeated my question.

174

She put one hand over her mouth to keep from crying and nodded her head so vigorously that her tears sprinkled over her skirt and on her hands and mine.

I asked her how old she was, and she controlled herself and smiled. "I am sixty-eight or sixty-nine, one of the two." She kept her sad, gray-green eyes on me, her head shyly cocked, and a slight appealing smile never left her lips.

I said, "Amparo, I want to thank you for taking care of him."

She looked down and nodded very fast as if she were consenting to a request. "Your father," she said, "was a very fine man." She kept nodding and looking into my face, both looking for traces of my father and waiting to be of service; a thousand things seemed to occur to her and, unable to give them speech, she communicated them with each emphatic nod and the tears which flooded her eyes.

I was as tongue-tied as she: I had long ago learned a set of manners which did not allow for this situation, which by omission of such a possibility taught me it must be avoided. But Galicia had begun to teach me its own code, and if, like Amparo, I could think of nothing to say, I could nod and smile with her and lean down and embrace her and kiss her again. Yet the release of tears, of which she was so easily capable, would not come; this last bastion of manly good manners would not yield, no matter how much I shared with Amparo, as we walked back into the tavern, the aching joy of a happy ending to my father's suffering.

In the tavern, Jose Sabell called out to me and pointed behind my shoulder. "There is Claudio!" I turned around and had no time or space to see anything; it was as if a wall had fallen on me and I closed my eyes as a reflex, while a tall bulk of a man hugged me and butted his head into mine. I brought up a hand and pushed against his shoulder to make a distance in which to see his face. Ruddy, long-faced with high cheekbones, deepset eyes, a wide slash of a mouth, Claudio was startlingly familiar. "Claudio!" I exclaimed. "You look like my sister and father!"

His strong arms dropped to his side; he wore a black beret, black pants and a clean, long-sleeved shirt neatly buttoned at the collar without a tie, and he looked at me with stolid dignity yet with all the hunger and happy surprise with which I had first gazed on Miamán. I went back to him and embraced him again and then introduced my wife and Rafael; each one went up to him, and Claudio was the first in Miamán whom Rafael chose, without urging, to kiss. Claudio grabbed his head and kissed him back and held him at arm's length and smiled approvingly. Then suddenly he walked brusquely past me to the counter and, as if separating himself from the crowd of people in the tavern, leaned on it and looked down.

"Claudio," I said, "I want to thank you . . ."

He shook his head and I stopped and he kept shaking his head, his mouth turned down at the corners like a gargoyle's. With one hand on the counter, grabbing it for support, he reached with the other into his back pocket

and brought out a handkerchief. He was sobbing noise-
lessly and he rolled the handkerchief into a ball and
scrubbed his cheeks with it; he was a tall, lean, strong
man, and every nail of his long powerful hands was out-
lined, as if with a penstroke, in deep black, by good clean
dirt.

"Claudio?" I said, and put a hand on his shoulder.

He looked up with eyes swimming in tears and there
was a supplicating look in them which seemed to ask for
forgiveness. I was so startled by the depth of suffering I
saw in them that I forgot what I wanted to say. Carlos
Andeiro took my elbow and brought me away. No one
looked at Claudio; his brother Gustavo Andeiro put the
broom away; Amparo smiled at me; my wife cried and
nodded to Ana Feijoo.

"Come," said Gustavo, "they are waiting at the house."
He waved the children away and closed the front door,
and Jose Sabell slapped me on the back. When Claudio
came over to me again to lead me out the back of the
tavern, his eyes were red but the suffering was under control.

They showed me the barns behind the tavern, the extra
orreo of Claudio's in the tavern yard, and as we walked in
a group past yards and narrow lanes to Claudio's home, I
got the sense from the quiet way in which he set the pace
for the group that Claudio was a man of considerable
achievement: he had gotten his own back in a way that
the little hunchback Asuncion was perhaps unaware. Carlos and Jose Sabell had told me that Claudio was the first
in Miamán to build a tall new house, and I expected

something grander than the first view I got of it in a close yard crowded with trees, though there were signs of affluence I could not recognize offhand: several cows, oxen, a pigpen with huge sows. Had I looked up from the open shed sheltering the door to the downstairs of the house, I would have seen that the old stones of the aldea houses at the base changed to blocks of good granite, and seen too the rows of open wooden windows looking out on the tops of the trees.

Claudio led me to the house like a feudal lord leading a friendly equal about his domain, and the cousins walking with us and those crowding inside acknowledged the relationship by the room they made for us, the way they made the children stand aside, and the way they looked at me for my reactions. The high point of the royal tour had been reached: we were being welcomed to his home, and every move I or my wife or son made and everything we said rippled into the laughter of others and their exclamations. A little woman broke through all this; she was tiny but her hands were large and rough and they grabbed my head and her face laughed at me. "Cousin, cousin, here you are at last!" she said, and someone said that she was Isabel, Claudio's wife. "This is your house," she added and laughed at herself: "Such as it is!"

I kissed her and she laughed and held on to one of my hands, and while she pointed out who were the other Andeiros and Fragas and Lopezes, she kept my hand in hers and brought it to her cheek and caressed it. "All right, all right," she yelled above everyone. "Upstairs with you all and let the women work!" She slapped Claudio on the back as if without her presence of mind the poor man would be lost, and he smiled tolerantly, used to her teasing, and led me past the activity of the kitchen to the wooden circular stairs at one end of the room.

I came out into a long bright room whose beamed ceiling was of light raw wood, its inner walls of plaster, and whose outside wooden walls were broken by long open windows; at one end double doors led out to a narrow three-foot ledge, from which you felt like leaping into the fresh shining air onto the thick treetops. I turned to look for my wife to see her reaction to this room every bit of whose surface had been made by hand, and saw a young girl leading her by the hand to the other end of the room and down a center hall; my wife kept turning her head and looking around, the way one does in those colonial houses in New England, not to miss some handiwork which shows the love of an artisan for his work.

The girl led her to the toilet, a walk-in closet of a room, all of it of the same light raw wood: a completely bare place whose function was recognizable only by a hole cut in the wooden floor. It smelled of fresh hay and you felt rather than knew that underneath there were animals. I never saw it, but Rafael did, and he told me later, "All I can say, Daddy, is that they must all be good shots!"

The long, air-filled room at the top of the stairs was furnished only with a solidly built table of the same wood as the walls; alongside it were sturdy benches and stools. On the plaster wall at one end of the table was a curious shelf on which Isabel had placed, as if on exhibition, the boxes of candies and pastries we had brought her from

Santiago. At another end of the room on another shelf was the only decoration in the room: a child's doll dressed in a long satin gown. It was covered with cellophane and obviously was never touched: no doubt Isabel's version of the Virgin.

By the time I had admired the place, looked out the windows, and been taken down the hall by Claudio to see the little bedrooms on either side of it, the room had become filled with cousins and children who though they did not always belong to them seemed to have the run of the house anyway. Isabel went to the wall near the double doors, opened the door of a built-in cupboard, and took out a photograph which she handed to Claudio. Everyone watched as he handed it to me. I recognized it immediately and so did my wife: my mother has a copy of it in her album at home. It was a studio picture of my mother sitting on a bench, my seven-year-old sister in a pageboy hairdo standing behind her, and me in front in short pants, a sailor blouse and hat with riband: a photograph specially taken to send to my grandmother when my father made that first trip to Miamán to be cured by the perfumed air which filled this upstairs room.

You had only to look at my sister and me to know that our whole beings were concentrated on the man who hid his head in the black snood of the camera, but our mother, carefully posed in three-quarters profile, seemed serenely by herself. Her dark, almond-shaped eyes looked away with gravity, and the wide, startling streak of gray hair, which began at the temple and disappeared into the large bun at the nape of her neck, set her apart even more.

Claudio said to me, "She is my only living aunt."

I wanted to say to him that she was not what she appeared in the photograph, that at twenty-six she was not this pre-Raphaelite young matron; she was a cigarmaker who ran home each day to cook, and spent her Sundays boiling clothes over a wood fire in the back yard. Instead I said, "You kept the picture all these years!"

Carlos Andeiro took the photograph from me and said, "That is a handsome, beautiful woman." I watched the photograph go from hand to hand in the room until it reached Amparo Noceda. "Oh yes, she is *guapa*," said someone at that moment—which means handsome, pretty, desirable—and Amparo nodded in agreement.

Claudio listened proudly to the compliments. "Grandmother always used to say that she was blessed to have such a daughter-in-law," he said, "who wrote her such affectionate letters."

Isabel, his wife, took the photograph from Amparo to put it away again. She laughed and said, "And one who sent her so much money!" She skipped and with a dancing motion went off to the cupboard.

We were there four hours and Isabel never sat down. Nor did she ever stop talking or teasing Claudio, and even with a platter of food in her hands she went through the steps of a jig or sang snatches of a song. "Oh Pepe, look at the serious man I married," she said once, pointing to Claudio. "He sits there solemn as a king when I should have married a gypsy!"

"Like me!" I said, and got up to dance with her. I had already drunk several bowls of thick Galician wine, and I was ready to do my own version of the sevillanas I had seen Andalusians dance in the streets of the Seville Fair. All it requires of the man—or so I thought at that moment—is that he hold himself very straight, lift his arms over his head, and clap his hands and stamp his heels. Instead of whirling round me snapping her fingers and stamping her heels, Isabel did a jig. We were a great success, and Claudio sat at the head of the table and enjoyed it.

When I sat down, Isabel danced over to the table to see if anyone's plate was empty, and watched my wife serve the course she had just brought up. "I see you are working," she said to her. "Whether they are serious like mine or a gypsy like yours, the men always let the women do the work."

There were two young girls downstairs to help her, but Isabel brought up all the platters of food herself and served the fifteen people at the table and distributed pieces to the children who came and went. There was no place at table for Isabel and when my wife protested that she must eat, she'd say, "Later, later, I have to see that you eat!"

First came the bread baked by her, enormous chunks of which she placed up and down the table. Then a potage of chick-peas made with their own sausages, and bowls of white rice. I took a second helping, thinking it the main course, and Carlos Andeiro and Jose Sabell, who sat across the table from me, warned me there was more to come. The second course was a huge Valencian paella; the third a casserole of rabbit and chicken cooked in a thick

brown sauce; fourth, platters of fried fish and potatoes;
fifth, slices of salt pork and two or three varieties of
sausages; sixth, a Galician specialty, *empanadas* of tuna, a
kind of pie made with pastry dough filled with tuna
cooked with onions and chopped olives in a tomato sauce.
Then the sponge cake baked in Santiago with eggs which
Isabel had sent from her own yard.

Claudio sat at the head of the table and I to his right.
He never got up and he never served the food, but his
eyes were everywhere, and while Isabel teased and
laughed, she also followed his gaze and complied. Occasionally a small child came and sat on his lap; he fed him
some food and then sent him off. The bowl of wine in front
of me was never anything but brimming, and I discovered that he had at the very outset commissioned Carlos Andeiro to see that it was kept full. There was, however, nothing pompous about Claudio, and occasionally I
would catch his face in repose and see that it became
immeasurably sad, as if he had once done something
which so shamed him that he had only to stop talking or
listening for it to return with full force.

I told him that Gustavo Andeiro had taken me to the
Asylum of the New Road, for I sensed that this had been
an order he had given his younger brother, and told him it
had made me happy to see that my father had spent his
last days in such a different kind of charity home from the
one I had imagined.

"I remember that we used to come in at the entrance,"
he said, "and that he was in the first room to the left. He
had a room all to himself."

"Then you used to visit him?"

"Yes, of course," he said, and looked at me, suspecting for the first time that I felt Father had been neglected. "Sometimes with my grandmother, sometimes with Amparo Noceda or my mother. We took turns."

"In those days you must have had to walk all the way to Santiago?"

"Yes," he said, and took out his balled-up handkerchief, "or go on horseback."

Down the table Gustavo Andeiro argued in a lively voice. It's the wine, I told myself, it has changed his character. "Claudio," I said, "do you know that you look remarkably like my sister?"

The Fraga cousins, dressed all in black and looking Amish, sat just beyond Carlos, and I heard one ask him what I did for a living. All those bowls of wine I had drunk seemed to make it possible for me to listen to every conversation at the table at the same time that I contemplated Claudio at my side. He nodded at me and said, "Your sister and I are the same age, I remember your father telling me."

Amparo called to him and me for the first time since I had talked to her outside Claudio's tavern. "Oh how he used to talk about his children!"

Carlos answered the Fragas in a whisper: "He is a man who knows many languages. He writes books . . . yes, books. You know, books to be read by people with the proper education, not by the likes of us."

I looked at Claudio and felt suddenly the same attraction those children felt who came to sit on his lap. He

looked at me with the protective air he extended to everyone at his table. "I used to like to visit him at the Asylum,"
he said, with tears in his eyes. "I was a boy and it was an
outing for me."

Ana Feijoo put down her fork and crossed herself. Then
with her fingers she stamped out the tears on her eyelids.

Isabel from nowhere appeared at Claudio's side and
slapped his shoulder. "No more sadness," she said. She extended her arms in front of her, ready for another jig, and
said to me, "Come." I got up and could not move my feet
but felt light and happy. She wore heavy, leaden country
shoes but she kicked her feet lightly and sang, "*Santa
Eulalia, the town where I was born/Whose romerias are
the gayest . . .*" Her face was flushed pink, and she held
her hands gracefully in front of her.

I took her hands in mine thinking I would show her a
square dance, and felt this time how hard and swollen
they were. From the little finger down to the wrist the
edges of her hands had the texture of wood, and the nail
of each thumb had been smashed and turned into little
black scabs. The flesh around each middle finger and forefinger was heavy and calloused, as if they had been used
for hammering, not picking up things. I did not attempt
the square dance, but bowed like a Madrileño and kissed
her hand.

"Ah, a real gypsy!" she exclaimed, and started on another trip down to the kitchen. At the stairs, just behind
Claudio, she touched his shoulder again. "No more sadness," she repeated, and catching my eye added, "That
man turns everything to sadness."

185

Claudio smiled broadly, happy with the day.

Between courses I would take one or two of the cousins over to the double doors and take a picture. The second time I did it I realized that a hush had fallen on the room and everyone had the look of a child anxious to be chosen. A photograph of oneself is a prized possession in Miamán, and Claudio very carefully and obliquely led the conversation round to Eliseo Carballo, the old man to whom I had been referred on our first day in Miamán. "You took photographs of his oxen and his granddaughters and his daughter," Claudio said. "He asked me if it would be possible to get a copy of those photographs."

When I used up the roll that I had brought with me, there was a chorus of disappointed ohs. Carlos Andeiro said to the Fragas, "He took a photograph of our oxen!" And the Fraga cousins looked at him with envy. "Not since Cousin Esperanza was here from Havana have we had pictures taken."

Asuncion arrived then and made a place for herself on the bench next to me. "There is room for you at the other end of the table," her brother said, but since Claudio said nothing, she did not budge, to show she had a claim on me based on closer acquaintance than the others. In her meek voice she said to me, "Pepe, I brought you salad because you said yesterday that you like it." Isabel placed the platter of lettuce and tomatoes and watercress in front of me, and I saw that these were the vegetables Asuncion had bought last night when I had thought that she loaded her basket at the grocery store only because I was paying.

"True, true," my wife said. "Vegetables in Spain are so delicious."

The Fragas looked at the platter curiously and so did Jose Sabell and Carlos Andeiro, and watched us serve ourselves.

"Speaking of Esperanza," said Carlos Andeiro. "What has happened to Fidel?"

"To Fidel?" I said, sure he meant Castro but giving myself time. "What has happened to him?"

"Well, Cousin Esperanza does not like him any more," Carlos explained. "When she first came in 1958 she liked him very much and then he won and she would send us magazines with his speeches—"

"Oh those speeches!" Ana Feijoo exclaimed and crossed herself. "We used to stay up until all hours of the night while one person read them aloud. Do you like his speeches? Oh what a marvel they were!"

"And now Cousin Esperanza says Fidel is no good," said Carlos. "What has happened?"

"I was in Havana in 1960," I said, "and most Cubans were very happy with him. There has been all that trouble with the United States since and many Cubans have left their country. I would say that people who owned businesses and big landowners have lost everything and are unhappy. But the poor farmers and the workers are happy with him."

Jose Sabell opened his eyes wide. "That is my idea of a good country, where the rich are bad off."

Carlos Andeiro screwed up his eyes and thought it over. "That explains it. Esperanza and her husband owned a big hardware store. They were doing very well by their own account. They had something to lose."

I looked at Claudio to see what he thought of all this. But it did not seem to interest him. He had a curious eye on the salad and I passed it to him. He smiled like a child who is going to try a new candy.

Carlos Andeiro said to me, "I think I have the explanation of why they talk badly about Fidel. It is the same thing as with Franco. They were both young men—you know that Franco was the youngest general in all Europe —and they both turned things upside down. It is jealousy, that is what it is, the jealousy of the old who do not want to see things changed by young men with new ideas. New ideas and the ability to do something about it. Don't you think that is the explanation?"

He waited for my answer, so I said, "It could be. I had not thought about it that way." And I looked at Claudio. He finished chewing and smiled. "It is very good," he said, and took more salad. "I like it."

Each time Claudio looked at me with appreciation he made me feel like a youngster. "Did my brother Gustavo tell you that I was determined to see you even if I had to go to Madrid?"

I nodded and smiled. His wife said, "He is just eager to get away from home, like all Galicians."

I asked him if he liked Madrid, and he said he had been there only once, many years ago. "With the Movement. I was a soldier and when the city fell I marched in. Those were bad days, I would like to see it now."

I looked away. Cousin Fraga's wife was reporting on me to Amparo. "Yes, everything, he seems to like everything," she said. "The wine too."

Amparo answered, "Oh, there is no food like the food in the aldea!"

I called to her: "You are right, there is none more delicious!"

Amparo covered her face with her hands.

"Oh, you are a gypsy," Isabel said. "You know how to flatter like an Andalusian."

I was able to look at Claudio again. He leaned forward and asked shyly, "Now tell me about my aunt, tell me how she is. Is she well?"

I told him and the table became quiet and listened.

"Do you think she would come and visit Miamán?" Claudio asked.

I said I thought she would like that very much, and there were murmurs of approval up and down the table.

"She is my only aunt," said Claudio. "I would like to see her very much. I would like to thank her."

"She was a wonderful woman," said Jose Sabell. "She tried so hard to get him back. She went to Havana, I know that."

This time Isabel did not joke. She took my hand and brought it up to her cheek and then kissed it.

My wife pointed to Ana Feijoo's wrist watch and asked her the time. She shook her head; the watch did not work: it was an ornament. "It is almost five," said Gustavo Andeiro. "The taxi will be at the road soon."

I got up and everyone with me. I heard little Asuncion say to the Fraga cousins, "Would you believe it, none of them owns a wrist watch!" I started to say goodbye but they told me they were all coming with us to the road.

"And you will not be coming back?" one of the Fraga cousins to whom I had barely spoken asked.

"Not this time," I said. "But I shall come back."

The women surrounded my wife, and the children Rafael, and the men took turns clasping me by the shoulders as we walked up the lane. Jose Sabell bent down once and grabbed one of my feet and held it over a thin clear stream and with one hand washed off the dung I had got on the shoe. They spoke only of the briefness of my visit, and asked when my ship would leave from Vigo; I did not say that I was broke, that I had to be in Vigo to receive a bank draft which was all the money I had and would just pay for the passage and the hotel bill in Vigo. I said, instead, that the week I would spend in Vigo before the ship left would have to be devoted to work; and they got that solemn respectful look as when I had told them I knew a little French and Italian.

Toward the road, the fields became bare; we were at the top of the mountain, and the taxi was waiting. "And you never sat down, Isabel," I said. I had an arm around her and I felt marvelous. I looked down toward the valley and made out the church where my father was baptized, the houses at whose edge stood the Principal House of the Andeiros. "How beautiful Miamán is!" I said. "The next time, if you do not ask me, I shall bring a sleeping bag and lie out in the fields!"

Then my wife and I began to kiss each one goodbye, and when I got to Claudio he grabbed me roughly again and I felt his head butting into my neck. "Claudio, Claudio," I said. "It has been a good day." And I saw all the others crying: Amparo held both hands to her face and as each tear came down she swept it off, Ana Feijoo covered hers with her apron, Jose Sabell wiped his face on his sleeve, and little Asuncion kept repeating, "Aiee, aiee!"

"I am going to come back," I said. "I swear to you in one year, maybe two, I shall be back to see you."

"God willing!" said Amparo. "Oh, God will be willing."

It became necessary to go back to each one once more and kiss them all goodbye again. The taxi driver looked away. Isabel began to walk up and down by the car, and suddenly yelled and waved her arms over her head. "I cannot bear it, I cannot bear it any longer! Get in the car and go," she said and rushed to me and kissed my hand again. "Go!"

I got in the front seat and watched Claudio who stood by the door looking down at me, his lips turned down at the corners. Behind him Carlos Andeiro wiped his eyes and kept one hand on Claudio's shoulder. The others got in back. "Ready?" said the driver.

"Wait!" said Claudio. "I am coming with you." He looked toward his wife; she had turned her back on the car. "Isabel," he called.

She raised an arm and nodded. Then she turned around. "Go," she said, "for you will not see him again—like all the others!" He got in and sat next to me and looked quietly down at his knees on each of which he had placed one of his long strong hands, and he did not smile or look around, like a child who has won a respite and will not endanger his victory.

The car started and I turned to take a last look. The men still watched and waved, but the women had covered their faces with their hands.

7

Walking around Santiago with Claudio that Sunday evening and the following day was less an action than a reminiscence: we were not doing, we were not reacting, we were already preparing to remember the day. We walked under the trees in the Horseshoe Park and thought how we would tell the folks back home about this; everything had happened, I believed, and now we were simply composing a sweeter parting, like a church mural of the painless death of a saint in which the principal, the bedside friends and hovering cherubs all smile beatifically. We went to the best restaurants and cafes in Santiago, looked at everything at one remove, and did all the things Claudio had never done on his trips to the city, so that it would acquire that quality for him too: he would return to Miamán on the workers' bus on Monday afternoon and lovingly tell Isabel where he walked and where he ate and what sweet things his cousins said.

Perhaps it was possible to make everything fall into the kind of place I envisioned for it because, as my wife said, being with Claudio was like spending time with a tree. He was inarticulate and solidly rooted, and he also gave shade and rest; he murmured at the things we did together as when a breeze stirs a tree's leaves, and when Rafael took his arm, Claudio welcomed him as if he were a bird who had come to rest. I took many photographs and we knew that two days hence they would be developed in Vigo, and thus before the week was out this prepared nostalgia would take shape.

Even the things that happened which were not of my doing conspired to sustain the mood until the moment we left. The last morning, after Claudio had returned to Miamán and left us loaded with gifts which he and Luz had bought for us and the family in Tampa, the two girls from Luz's aldea who worked in El Gran Derby showed up at our hotel. They brought a slab of ham and a cheese which Luz sent Rafael because she had noticed the previous evening, when we sat at a cafe facing the Horseshoe Park, that he ate the thin slices of ham and cheese with gusto. We made the girls come up to our room, and after much urging, they sat on the edge of a bed and shyly holding one another's raw red hands began to reminisce.

"Oh sir, what a surprise it was," said the older one, "that day when you walked in!"

"And you ordered coffee and we did not have it . . ."

"So then, sir, you ordered Pepsi-Cola and oh the look on

the master's face when you said you were his carnal cousin from Cuba! Who can forget such an event!"

I did not correct them: the myth had taken shape and I would not tamper with details. They had not been at the bar when we arrived at El Gran Derby but upstairs working, but the story now belonged to them, not me.

The gifts were so many that we had to delay our leaving for Vigo a few hours to get them properly packed, and after we checked our things at the station, we still had an hour and a half. We went, of course, to our favorite cafe facing the Horseshoe Park, ordered our usual drinks and the tiny platters of fried squid rings and snails in red sauce, and we watched the midday paseo beginning to form. The women carrying their shopping on their heads interested us most and so we almost missed Soledad Sanchez Miguez, whom we had met on our first visit to El Gran Derby and who had entrusted me with the job of finding her father in New York.

I ran after her when my wife's gesturing did not catch her attention—we were seated at a bourgeois cafe and it would not have occurred to her to look at those tables for someone she knew—and she came happily to join us. She had never been at such a fine cafe, but she sat down with great self-possession and ordered an anise from the waiter with no change in her usual manner. When friends saw her with us and called out greetings, she responded with a smile which said, Go ahead and be surprised but here I am, I am as good as anybody else.

She wore the same shawl tucked in at her waist and the same pendant earrings. "I am in the city today with my son-in-law," she said, "because today the union is holding a hearing to determine whether my son-in-law was innocent when he knocked out the foreman's tooth the day he was provoked. He was suspended from his job and today he finds out whether he gets it back or not." She gave a loud peal of laughter, took a sip of the strong anise, and said, "Holy Virgin, you are going to think we are a fighting family!"

"Did you advise him on how to comport himself at the hearing?" I asked.

She tapped me on the shoulder and winked. "I see you remember I know a thing or two about such matters. Do not think I have not advised him—you have to know, I told him, where to stand when you grab the donkey's tail!"

When we told Soledad that we were leaving for Vigo, she said, "I was in Vigo once, to see my mother off to Argentina. That was six years ago and she used to live with us, but my older sister sent for her. They were both working at good jobs and my mother could help by taking care of the grandchildren. Not that we did not want her, for I made my husband respect her. Listen, I used to tell him, you can always get yourself another woman and if I want there is no trouble finding a man, but a mother cannot be replaced. So you can be assured that it was not a question of her not being wanted with us.

"I went to Vigo and sat in the ship by her side, in a large room where the women had their beds. I kept looking at her, for I was afraid that I might forget what she looked like, and I was the last person to leave the ship.

They kept announcing that visitors had to leave and my mother finally said, Come, daughter, you must leave now. First I kissed her on the forehead, then on the lips. I kissed her hands too and I could not leave her yet. So I got down on the floor and kissed her feet and she began to cry but it made me feel better. Not then, but later, I was glad I kissed her feet, for when I walked off that ship nothing could make me feel better."

We walked away from the cafe in different directions, but after half a block Soledad caught up with us. "Listen, when you find my father in New York, go see him at work first—the Casa Ford, remember—because no doubt he has another woman and may not want her to know about his family here. Tell him he can write to me as if I were his sister or some such relative. And if he wants to send me a gift, tell him I would like earrings—the kind that hang!"

Two days later, at our favorite cafe in Vigo, we looked at all the snapshots we had taken of those last two days in Santiago. There was Soledad leaning across the table talking to me; Claudio and Gustavo and Luz standing outside El Gran Derby; Claudio walking across the wide expanse of the Plaza del Obradoiro with an arm on Rafael's shoulders; Claudio sitting next to the driver of the bus smiling goodbye. I made a space on the tiny table, wrote a note, and addressed an envelope to Claudio; he would have them in another day and with them could round out the experience as we were doing.

I wondered, I wondered, for until that afternoon in Vigo I had held back from my wife one small exchange—it could not have lasted more than thirty seconds—that took place between Claudio and me on our last day with him. I wondered if he had had to make as great an effort as I to put it out of mind and pursue as determinedly as I a happy ending to our pilgrimage to Miamán. We had been walking in the Horseshoe Park a few paces ahead of my wife, Luz and Rafael, and our conversation consisted, as if by common agreement, of questions to which there were only pleasant answers. Sometimes Claudio used a Galician word or two which I could not figure out, but so long as I got the drift I nodded and smiled.

We had made the turn and could now see the enchanting postcard view of the cathedral through the break in the trees, and I absentmindedly nodded at something Claudio said. When I looked at him to point out the view, I saw that he looked embarrassed and upset, and it first occurred to me that he thought my automatic response condescending, but I recalled that he had asked a question and my nod may have been the wrong answer. "I am sorry, Claudio," I said, "I did not understand."

He made an effort to say it all in Castilian. "You saw the house where your father was born? Carlos and Jose Sabell said you specially wanted to see it."

"Oh yes," I replied. "I took a photograph of it to show my mother and sister."

He did not look at me when he said, "That house belonged to our grandmother and your father and it now belongs to my brother Gustavo. Did you know that it belonged half to your father and half to our grandmother?"

"No," I said, "but I suppose it must have."

"Your father sold his half to our grandmother before he died and he signed papers when that happened. I hope Gustavo showed them to you, for it was all legally done."

I stopped looking at him and said quickly, "I did not see them and I am not interested in that. It is not any of my business anyway."

I made an enormous effort and dammed up that bit of conversation. "Look at the view," I said, "look at the cathedral." I was not going to leave Santiago with my feelings about my Galician family again unresolved; I stopped and waited for the others to catch up. "Look how beautiful Santiago is!" I said to them, and saw on Claudio's face a look of relief and gratitude: he had worked himself up to tell me and it had all gone so easy and well.

Not for me: I had only to recount it to my wife in Vigo for Claudio's story to flood and submerge the whole time. "Why did he tell me that?" I asked. "What made him think I wanted to know that?" And I had only to ask that question, to go just one logical step beyond Claudio's confession, for it all to become clear: "My God!" I said. "Do you realize that I am the legal heir! They must have been scared of me . . ."

Everything which had been puzzling and disturbing in my visit was explained by this fact to which my cousins must have given such importance. My father's sister Remedio was illegitimate and, it followed, everything my grandmother owned should come to me via my father's legitimacy. That little house and its lands to which my grandmother moved when she married my father's father should have come down to me. My father's father! He was a total blank. No one in Miamán mentioned him and all my questions about him were unanswered. When I asked about his family, I had been told there were no more of them in Miamán.

And the land in Nodar? No, I thought, that must have been Claudio's father's land or he must have bought it when he married Remedio. Then I remembered the little hunchback Asuncion in the yard of the Andeiro house, on our first day in Miamán, explaining how my grandmother had moved from Fuenfría to Nodar. She had said Aunt Dolores had bought lands in Nodar and then she had become alarmed and said the old woman had bought them because she had to. Had Asuncion become alarmed when she volunteered that information because at that moment they were all wondering if I had come to Galicia to claim my property?

"Oh, it's true what they say about Galicians, after all," I said to my wife. "They're very sly."

But it was a poor joke and would not relieve me of my feelings. My good cousin Claudio, *he* knew the extent of the duplicity and that was why, when with us, his face in repose took on such a sad expression.

"Your mother sent your grandmother fifteen dollars a month," said my wife. "Can you imagine how much money that must have been then? It's a lot now."

I remembered Claudio's wife Isabel, when the others praised my mother for her beauty and goodness, adding truthfully, "And she sent her so much money." That money must have made it possible for my grandmother to buy lands in Nodar. What a boon my sick father had been for the old woman! Whenever I had asked about their aunt Dolores, the cousins had said she was a lively woman and laughed, but the word in Spanish could mean lively and it could also mean lively and clever and wily. Little Asuncion had said that the old woman had stopped writing because she was afraid my mother and my sister and I would descend on her and she, an old woman with a sick daughter and two small grandchildren, would have to take care of us too. And so she had cut us off.

But it had not been so simple, I could see now, and we stayed in that cafe in Vigo until I thought I had worked it all out. It was not until Remedio died and the old woman was left with Claudio and Gustavo that she made her decision to answer no more of my mother's letters. If everything she owned belonged to me, how were those two boys to live? Without land no one can eat in Galicia, and those two boys were right there: they were truly her very own. My father was dead, there was no other tie to us. If my mother could have sent her money all those years, we must not need that land like her two boys. She made her terrible decision, but when she was in her eighties and everything seemed to have worked out all right, she began to worry about my sister and me and to moan about what could have become of us.

"And look what became of us!" I said. "I descend on Miamán like an American millionaire traveling for fun, friendly and interested, delighted to find cousins, and not a word about my property. Poor Claudio, no wonder he seems sad and cannot look at us without crying."

The repentant, sorrowing old woman had left Claudio with this miserable burden, all due to a legalism which counted for nothing with me. It was Claudio, no doubt, who when he came into the city looking for us stirred his brother Gustavo to make inquiries about where my father was buried. Gustavo had not inherited the guilt: he was too young then and he had traveled and now had a business and consequently didn't bother to bring out any dubious papers to show me the land was legally his. Not when I hadn't made the slightest request. So Claudio alone felt the obligation to do something about it and had screwed up his courage and broached the subject in the Horseshoe Park.

"Poor Claudio, poor Claudio." I shook my head, thinking of what he must have gone through. "I'm sorry I didn't let him talk more and go into the whole thing. I would have had the chance, then, to tell him that the land belongs to those who work it."

My wife smiled. "That sounds like a revolutionary slogan, and Claudio is so conservative that he would probably not agree with you."

Still, I was sorry I had already sealed the envelope with the snapshots and the note to Claudio, for I might have found a way to tell him. Poor Claudio, poor grandmother: Soledad wanted pendant earrings from America but she also equally wanted to find her father, while they had wanted their land and security and also wanted me and my sister and mother. Perhaps not equally, but enough. When we left the cafe, we stopped by the post office and mailed the letter to Claudio. It was a proper ending, I thought, a good ending.

Before I fell asleep that night, I realized I had the sequence of events wrong and that my grandmother *had* been sly, that she had prepared the inheritance for Claudio and Gustavo long before she stopped writing my mother. First, she had gotten Father to sign over the house to her and, to be doubly sure, she had inscribed him in the Asylum of the New Road as a bachelor. But why had she continued to write for two years after Father died? Greed, I decided: I was very angry with the old woman by then. Mother still sent a little money with her replies; I know that when the old woman's last letter arrived announcing Remedio's death, Mother sent her money to help pay for the burial. Did she buy more land with it?

Why, then, did she stop writing when she did? Father was two years dead. She was lively and clever and wily: was she afraid to push her luck? Then I remembered Amparo Noceda and was tempted to give the old woman a rationale which spoke well for her: Amparo lived with her, worked for her and took care of the boys. Claudio had said to me, "There is no repaying Amparo for what she did for us. She manages now: I give her a place to stay and she goes out to work as a day laborer to make the few pennies she needs. But we can never really repay her!" So perhaps the old woman decided, out of a sense of justice, that while she had Amparo she could not also call on Mother for help.

But it wouldn't stick: I could not believe in such sensibilities in an old peasant woman. And it occurred to me that in all this it was Amparo Noceda who had been most ill-used. She had no relatives in this world and at sixty-eight—or sixty-nine?—she went out to do odd jobs to pay her way, and she did not own for a gala Sunday a shirt with all its buttons. No, the old woman stopped writing because when the brother who wrote her letters died, there was no one in Miamán to whom she would trust the knowledge that she had a daughter-in-law and grandchildren in America. How often, I wondered, had the photograph of Mother and my sister and me been taken out and shown?—for on that Sunday at Claudio's home everyone seemed to be looking at it for the first time.

It took me two days to make my peace with the old woman, and on the third morning I woke up and said, "She was old Mother Courage, that's who she was, and if I'd been her I would have done the same—more credit to her!" Vigo seemed all the more inviting for my decision, and we took a trolley ride I had been putting off. For fifteen cents each we boarded an electric trolley which left every hour from the plaza facing our cafe and ended up an hour and a half later at the town of Bayona down the coast. Fifteen minutes from the plaza, it leaves the city and winds along the bay, through fishing villages and farm fields, and skirts beaches all the way to Bayona. There were black-kerchiefed women in the fields bent over working, but no men: they were at work in West Germany, France, Belgium, as in my grandmother's day they were in the Americas.

The town of Bayona is in a tiny cove of a harbor, and when we got off the trolley, we walked on the main street along its edge until it became a highway bordering the coast of the Atlantic. As soon as we turned away from the bay, the winds of the ocean hit us, and we doubled slightly and squinted to look at the shore; the road was uphill and the oceanside stood high over enormous rocks all the way down to the water. There were fine, bourgeois homes along the road facing the sea, and at the highest point there was a pine and eucalyptus forest where stood the Virgin of the Rock hewn out of the same gray stone piled along the shore. It was this strong wind, I liked to imagine, which drove one of Columbus' ships into the bay of Bayona, on their return trip from America, and so it was this little fishing town which was the first to hear of the discovery of America.

"Not the discovery of America, Daddy," said Rafael, "but of the new route to India."

The same strong winds pushed us back down the road and into town. We were the only people there with nothing to do, and we sat at a cafe and had a drink before we took the trolley back. Even the second time around, the ride was extraordinary, and we joked about telling no one about it, so that it wouldn't be ruined: it would be our "in" place. At a cove with fishing boats two men got on who had been drinking and they sang and did a few steps in the aisle until a young Civil Guard got on and stopped them with angry words. Everyone got set faces and looked away, and I suddenly became depressed and disgusted with Spain: accursed land, it rejects all gaiety.

And the mood gave me leave to think about my father in a new way: as the man who signed the papers selling his share of his home to his mother. Could such a transaction have taken place? Did he bargain? What was his price? Room and board and care for the two years before he went to the hospital? I laughed: that was not my father. But how did I know? Life is hard and he was at the old woman's mercy.

I tried to think of other than the obvious explanation: that he no more cared about such legalities than I did. He signed the papers to do simply what was just. To make his mother and sister happy. Of course. Yet he was a Miamán boy—what if he believed in his very bones, as Galicians do, that the only salvation you can leave your sons is land? And, believing that, signed the papers and shared in the decision: for Claudio and Gustavo, against my sister and me. Then signed in at the Asylum as a bachelor.

I took advantage of the noise the trolley made as we entered the paved city streets to talk aloud without being heard. I said, "I think I am going mad."

At the hotel was a letter from Claudio written with a stubby pencil and great care. Although it was on lined paper, each line of writing climbed to the right, a sign, a handwriting fortuneteller once told me, of well-being and optimism. *I read Isabel your letter,* he wrote, *and she complains that she has such a kind cousin and he is going away and all she saw of you was one afternoon so do not be surprised if she shows up at your hotel on Friday.*

Good, I thought, I'll talk to her; she won't think I'm so kind and good. I won't be angry, I'll simply let her know

that I understood what they meant when they said Dolores Andeiro was lively and clever and wily. But it must
be a joke of Claudio's: how could Isabel come all the way
to Vigo alone? Nevertheless, after the morning walk next
day, we stayed in our rooms at the hotel and waited and
at noon the phone rang and I was told there was someone
downstairs who claimed I was his cousin.

I did not take the slow lift; I ran down two flights of
stairs. By the desk stood Claudio, so carefully dressed he
wore a tie; he smiled and at the same time was guarded,
as if in this first-class hotel in the big city of Vigo I might
deny I was, as he had told them at the desk, his cousin.
He had told them I was his cousin to explain his presence
in a hotel where he did not belong, and I saw this the moment he smiled, so I was more exuberant than I'd ordinar-
ily be in a hotel lobby.

"And Isabel? You said Isabel was coming."

He talked very quietly. "She is with the others outside,"
he said. I said, Well, let us go get them; but he held my
arm and said, They would rather wait for us outside. I insisted we get Isabel and bring her upstairs to my wife
first. "You have been traveling, you must rest a moment,"
I said, and went out into the street. They weren't there,
nor at the tables in the hotel's sidewalk cafe which extended to the street corner. Then Claudio walked down to
the corner and I followed him. On the side street down
the block stood a group of peasants in a sea of bundles:
Carlos and Ana Feijoo, Luz and her little girl, and Isabel.

It took considerable urging to get them in the hotel. I
put the women and little Lucita in the lift and rang the

third-floor button for them, and Carlos and Claudio and I walked up the stairs. They had left Miamán before sunrise, met Luz and her little girl in the Santiago station, and taken the first train to Vigo; they had come to spend a couple of hours with us and then go back. "No, you will stay overnight," I said, "I shall convince the women." But I could not find them; they were not in the small lounge in front of the lift, nor down the corridors, and then it occurred to me to open the doors of the lift. They were still standing in it, afraid to open the doors.

"What a marvel!" said Isabel, and stepped out.

I told her and the others that they were going to spend the night in the hotel and return to Santiago the next day. Ana Feijoo said she would never be able to fall asleep there; I assured her that it was comfortable. Isabel, who had been holding my hand and kissing it as we walked down the corridor, stopped and said with her witty frankness, "Pepe, we are uneducated people from the aldea— we were ashamed to walk into the hotel, so you can imagine how the idea of staying in it strikes us!"

My wife worked very hard to make them sit on the bed in our room and showed the women the bathroom, for they had been traveling for hours. They stood in the doorway of the bathroom and looked inside with awe and never made a move to use it. "That is a shower," said Luz, the city girl, to the others.

"It is too good for us, Pepe," Isabel said. "We would never be able to stay here, even if we had the time." And she sat on the bed and told us what they wanted to do with the day, interrupting herself only to kiss my wife or take my hands and bring them to her cheeks and caress them. "No, no, no," she said to my suggestion that we all have lunch in the hotel dining room.

Ana Feijoo said, "We brought a few little things, enough to have a bite."

Carlos said, "We thought we could go to a park or a beach nearby and have a bite and talk and then we would go home."

I suggested we still have lunch in the hotel and then go to a beach across the bay and there have the bite. "I have not given up hope that you will stay overnight."

Isabel came right to the point. "To tell you the truth, Pepe, we would not appreciate the food they serve in a place like this."

"All right," I said. "But you will stay tonight. After all, have you been in Vigo before?"

Luz shook her head, so did Isabel and Carlos. Claudio had been in Vigo twice. Ana Feijoo said nothing, and when I asked her, she burst into tears. "Ana was here to see her brother off," Luz explained, and she patted Ana Feijoo's hand. Ana was wearing the kerchief with a little bit of color in it and the memory of her brother must have been more painful on the day she had broken her mourning.

But she managed to smile at me and said, "Asuncion said to me, You go, Ana, you must not miss this opportunity, and she stayed to do the work. That was so nice of Asuncion."

The half hour in the hotel room became a tug of war between us on whether they would stay the night, and when I persuaded them to leave some of their bundles in our rooms, I thought I had won the first battle. Downstairs, the manager recommended we take the ferry to the other side of the bay where there were many beaches, and we walked along the waterfront with our bundles, my cousins stopping to buy fruit at the stands, marveling at the ships, their eyes alert to everything that happened and every person who passed. Except for Isabel, they were reserved and watchful in their manner: Isabel had congratulated the chambermaids at the hotel on how well they kept the place, at the ferry's open top deck she announced to everyone that this was her first time on the water, and when the ferry sounded its loud horn to depart, she screamed.

"And you have traveled all day to give us this surprise," my wife said, "to say goodbye."

Isabel sat between us and said, "Yes, yes, for we do not believe your husband's promises. He says he will return next year or the next, but I know him, he is a gypsy." She took one of my hands, and while the other passengers watched and Claudio looked over the side with embarrassment, she sang in a small sweet voice:

> Buenos Aires, Buenos Aires,
> For Buenos Aires
> I leave tomorrow and if I marry
> I'll not return.
>
> Buenos Aires, Buenos Aires,
> They say it's good in Buenos Aires,

From the ages of fifteen to twenty
They leave and then forget to return!

We had very little time, for at the ferry's ticket booth
Claudio had asked about the time schedule, and they told
us the last ferry we could take back was at five thirty
since the last train from Vigo to Santiago left at seven. We
argued about this and about who would pay for the fruit
and the ferry tickets, and when we got off at the little
town of Cangas on the other side of the bay, I ran ahead
down the breakwater, for I knew that they would object
to my hiring a taxi. Claudio ran after me when he found
out what I planned to do, and Isabel yelled, "We shall be
offended if you do that!"

But I convinced them we had little time to waste walking out of the town to find a beach, and a taxi driver told
me he knew a place where we could picnic under the trees
right by a beach. He took us to the beach in two groups,
the women first, and when Claudio, Carlos and I arrived
there we walked across a cove sparkling with white sand
and rocks to where, under pine trees, on a little height
above the beach, the women had spread out the little bite
they had brought from Miamán.

Isabel had taken off her skirt so as not to wear it out,
and danced about in her slip serving everyone as she had
done at home. The little bite turned out to be huge
amounts of ham, sausages, tongue, pigs' feet, fried fish,
bread, a gallon of wine, cakes, apricots, pears and pastry
twists sprinkled with sugar. The pine glade and the little
beach below were all ours, but even if they had not been,

it would not have stopped Isabel from singing and dancing. Luz turned out to have a strong high voice, and she
sang for us while Isabel danced.

"Ah, we are nothing, nothing at all," said Isabel when
we complimented them. "You should hear Ana."

But when we asked Ana Feijoo to sing, her eyes filled
with tears. "I accompany you in your sentiments, I am
glad that you sing and dance," she said. "But I cannot today."

Claudio took out a package and called Rafael. Isabel
signaled to us to watch as Rafael unwrapped it: it was a
shiny red bagpipe with yellow tassels, a gift they were
very proud of. Claudio played it for Rafael and Isabel
called to me, "Take a photograph of him, for the love of
God! I will give five thousand pesetas for it to show in the
aldea. Do you know what a serious man he is!"

Whenever I tried to take a picture of her, she brought
the shoulder bone of a pig to her face like a fan, or put it
to her lips like a lollipop. She got my wife off the ground
and the two of them danced a jig while Luz sang and
Claudio played the bagpipe he brought Rafael. There was
no time for conversation, for exchanging facts: everything
was presence and feeling, and the glade in the mottled
sunlight was like the wine we drank, shimmering with
highlights and cool shade. When the taxi appeared on the
other height beyond the beach, I said, "I shall miss not
being at your romeria in Miamán."

"We wanted to give you a little taste of it," Isabel said
and kissed my hand.

212

I pointed down to the beach where my wife had gone for a few moments to lie in the sun. "That is very typically American," I said. "We like to lie in the sun."

"Oh, Cousin Elena!" Ana Feijoo exclaimed. "She is as good as a piece of bread."

"Do you know that, you gypsy?" said Isabel. "Your wife is not ashamed of ignorant people from the aldea like us."

"A saint," said Luz, "she is a saint."

The taxi driver knew us well by then, and he wanted to take us to the whale yard of the cannery plant. "It is the biggest cannery plant in Spain!" he said. "You cannot leave Cangas without seeing it. First, I shall take the women and they will hold the ferry."

While we waited for the taxi to return for us, I made a last attempt with Claudio and Carlos to convince them to stay one night in Vigo. "We are family, so you will forgive me if I say something wrong," I said. "If the problem is money, I want you to know I have it."

Claudio shook his head. "We have left the old people to do the work. They can do it for one day but for more than that it would be wrong. But you command, cousin, if you say we must, then we will do what you say. But it would be wrong."

I gave in. "Still, it would give me such pleasure to take you out this evening in Vigo. We could climb up to the top of El Castro and look down on the city."

Their faces were full of doubt about their decision. Then Carlos said, "Pepe, let me tell you, this day has been wonderful enough. Already the women have seen and done things they never imagined they would come near in their entire lives. Think of it, at this very moment they are seeing the whale yard of the famous Masso plant!"

The whale yard fascinated Carlos and Claudio. We looked at the men in hip boots cutting up the carcasses of a couple of whales and trampling over the chunks of meat in spiked shoes. Blubber was being boiled in enormous cauldrons and the pieces of whale and the pop-art entrails lay around the yard by the water; in the sea, a dead whale, kept afloat by air which had been pumped into it, waited its turn. The driver said, "It does not taste like fish, you know, more like chicken," and Claudio and Carlos nodded and stored away that bit of information.

As we drove up the breakwater in the taxi, Isabel called to us from the open deck of the ferry, "Do not worry, I would not let it go without you!" And she made me sit with her and drew my wife to her other side. "So many things happened," she said, "that I did not get to say the things we planned to say." She took my hand preparatory to saying it. "When you get to your country, you are going to see your sister first?"

I nodded.

"I want you tell her from me and Claudio—Claudio, come here!—I want you to tell her that whenever you or she wants it there is land for you and her in Miamán. There is land for you to build a house of your own and for her to build a house of her own."

I explained to my wife that they were giving us land in Miamán to come and build a house and live there. "Isabel," I said, and pulled Claudio's sleeve so he would listen, "I cannot adequately express what this means to me, I really cannot tell you."

She slapped my hand and exclaimed, "Do not make too much of it, man! You cannot sell land in Miamán, nobody wants it, so it is not very much of an offer!" And she got up and began to do a jig.

"We shall come and stay with you," I said.

"Never mind those promises," she said. "Come and dance with me now."

"I shall show you a dance we did when I was a young man," I said, and while she lifted her feet in the jig, I did a couple of steps of the Lindy. Everyone in the ferry laughed, even Claudio; he had stopped looking out at the water when his wife embarrassed him.

We took two taxis to the hotel, for there was little time, and the women went up to get the bundles. When the driver wasn't listening, I said to Claudio, "I tried to thank you before, but I did not do a good job. I want you to know that meeting you and spending this time with you has made my father seem somehow less dead."

Claudio twisted his hands together. "And my mother and grandmother, they have all come back too. For this while."

Carlos looked at us with his enormous black eyes and nodded.

"They did not bring down the bundles," I said when I saw the women coming back.

My wife came over to our taxi. "The bundles upstairs are all gifts and more gifts," she said. "Fabrics, wines, cognacs, souvenir dolls. They have even canned the sausages and pork slabs from their own farm!"

In the railroad station, Isabel, Ana Feijoo and Luz held my arms to keep me from paying for their tickets. Claudio bought third-class tickets, of course; the last wooden car on the train with high, uncomfortable wooden benches, but all, of course, grander than the accommodations at home in Miamán. We went in with them, for there was plenty of time, and Claudio had something more to say.

"About my aunt," he said.

"My mother?"

"Yes, my aunt," he said. "Do you believe she would like to come and visit us in Miamán?"

I nodded. "Oh yes."

"Then let me tell you what Isabel and I have been discussing. If you would put her on a boat to Vigo, we would come and get her and take her to Miamán. And when it came time for her to return we would pay her passage back. She would not need any money while she is here, for we would get her whatever she needs. You will tell her that?"

I said I would tell her that. "You are a very good man, Claudio," I said.

"She is my aunt, my only aunt," said Claudio, and his eyes filled with tears.

"Come, no more of that," said Isabel harshly. "You are getting sentimental and it makes me nervous that they are still on the train and it may start."

I laughed. "So we would go to Santiago and say goodbye there and then you would come again to Vigo and say goodbye!"

Ana Feijoo began to cry. We kissed them all and went down to the platform. There was no one else in their car and Isabel and Luz and Ana Feijoo talked to us from the window. Carlos and Claudio stood on the viewing platform of the train and talked to Rafael. Isabel held out her arms and with her rough hands took one of mine. "As you stand there," she said, "you remind me of your grandmother, Dolores Andeiro. It is not that you look exactly like her, but there is something about your forehead and eyes. Yes, there is something . . ."

Ana Feijoo nodded and bit her lips.

"Did you know her, Ana?" I asked.

She nodded and covered her face with her hands because she was ashamed to cry. "Heavens, you must not cry, woman," said Isabel. "This is a happy day." And then the train moved and a terrible look came over Isabel's face, as if her foolish words had set the train off. "Oh damned God!" she moaned and pulled back from the seat and ran out to the viewing platform with Claudio.

The train stopped again, and I held up both hands to Claudio. "Cousin Claudio!" I said. "Cousin Claudio!" And like a good Galician I began to cry. Isabel tried to speak but she seemed to choke and only a thin wail came out. Behind me, my wife and Rafael called, "Adios, adios, adios!"

I ran a few steps with the train, and while Isabel held one arm over her face and waved with the other, Claudio took out a handkerchief and waved it and leaned his tall body against the train and sobbed. "Cousins!" I yelled, and before the train picked up speed I saw them both stare at me, afraid to blink, just as I would not blink, in order to see through our tears. "I promise I shall come back!"

I saw them become small before my eyes and I took out my handkerchief and waved it each time Claudio waved his. Then I wiped my face with it, happy to have cried. Happy I had not asked them any questions, happy their presence was enough. Sometimes, of course, I wonder, I speculate again about the past Claudio and I inherited and I feel once more that hurt which makes me think I am going mad. It is then I treasure that last goodbye like a talisman: their tears and mine make everything right. In this terrible land of necessity I need to believe human goodness supervenes.